READING FUTURE

CHANGE

2

Susan Ludwig · Kelli Ripatti
Tamara Wilburn · Lucas Foster

Table of Contents

Scope & Sequence

Subject	Unit	Title	Word Count	Reading Skill	Vocabulary Skill
SCIENCE	1	Artificial Limbs	161	Sequencing	**Antonyms** open: close natural: artificial heavy: light past: future
SCIENCE	2	Winners Wear Red	160	Main Idea & Details	Conjunction **if**
SCIENCE	3	Noise Pollution	164	Reviewing	**-tion** construc**tion** informa**tion** ac**tion** solu**tion**
SCIENCE	4	Understanding the Heart	168	Sequencing	**keep** + A + B
LITERATURE	5	Hypertext Literature	169	Classifying	**Same Singular and Plural Form** series fish sheep deer
LITERATURE	6	Types of Writing	170	Classifying	**Compound Words** newspaper armchair eyeball firefighter pancake
LITERATURE	7	The Power of Poetry	170	Cause & Effect	**Adverbs of Time** early late then today
LITERATURE	8	A Positive Thinker: *Anne of Green Gables*	164	Main Idea & Details	**-sion** deci**sion** discus**sion** conclu**sion** expre**ssion**
ECONOMICS	9	Digital Money	168	Main Idea & Details	adverb + comparative even far much a lot
ECONOMICS	10	The History of Money	168	Sequencing	**Irregular Past Tense Verbs** understood had became made lost
ECONOMICS	11	The Stock Market	168	Sequencing	**co-** **co**operate **co**write **co**worker **co**-owner
ECONOMICS	12	Credit Cards	169	Summarizing	**Compound Nouns** credit card middle school paper clip swimming pool
MATH	13	The Math of Faces	169	Main Idea & Details	Words as Nouns and Verbs face hand answer work
MATH	14	Cooking with Math	169	Sequencing	**Counting Words With *of*** 1 cup of flour two bowls of soup a glass of milk three slices of cake
MATH	15	Measurement Systems	168	Cause & Effect	Imperial and Metric Measurements 1 pound: 0.454 kg (kilograms) 1 inch: 2.54 cm (centimeters) 1 mile: 1.609 km (kilometers)
MATH	16	Measuring Big Animals in the Wild	170	Sequencing	**-ist** scient**ist** art**ist** pian**ist** tour**ist** journal**ist**

Vocabulary				Project	21st Century Skills	
artificial respond	fake rotating	replace extend	light stairs	Thankful for Our Arms and Legs	Critical Thinking	Collaboration
uniform outcome	simply opponent	recent automatically	competition influence	Colors and Feelings	Critical Thinking	Communication
silent traffic	realize construction	common serious	health reduce	Quiet Places	Critical Thinking	
vital empty	organ pump	necessary vitamin	chamber oxygen	A Healthy Heart	Critical Thinking	Communication
device format	interact central	hyperlink storyline	participate series	Make Your Own Story!	Creativity	Communication
purpose event	emotion newspaper	contain magazine	plot fact	Favorite Literature Types	Collaboration	Communication
proverb reflect	early surface	late soil	consider appreciate	Read More Poems	Critical Thinking	Communication
orphan instead	elderly positive	disappointed attitude	arrive firmly	An Interesting Character	Critical Thinking	Creativity
cash method	check recently	coin increasingly	card security	Create Digital Money	Collaboration	Communication
throughout introduce	exchange value	service stamp	commodity convenient	Design New Money	Critical Thinking	Creativity
stock profit	own investor	cooperate hire	increase improve	Start Your Own Business	Creativity	Communication
borrow bill	due purchase	interest password	fundamental responsible	Cash or Credit Card	Collaboration	Communication
feature width	program individual	recognize identify	geometry crowd	Facial Features	Critical Thinking	Creativity
aid double	particularly tricky	kitchen culinary	vanilla calculation	Using Fractions	Critical Thinking	Collaboration
widely unfortunately	currently trouble	mile agency	pound fail	Using Different Measurements	Critical Thinking	Communication
tool figure out	creative approximate	manual proportion	collect estimate	Other Ways to Measure	Critical Thinking	Creativity

How to Use

Student Book

WARM-UP

A short reading and questions with an impactful image helps students activate their background knowledge and approach the topic.

NEW WORDS

Learn the meaning of important vocabulary with pictures.

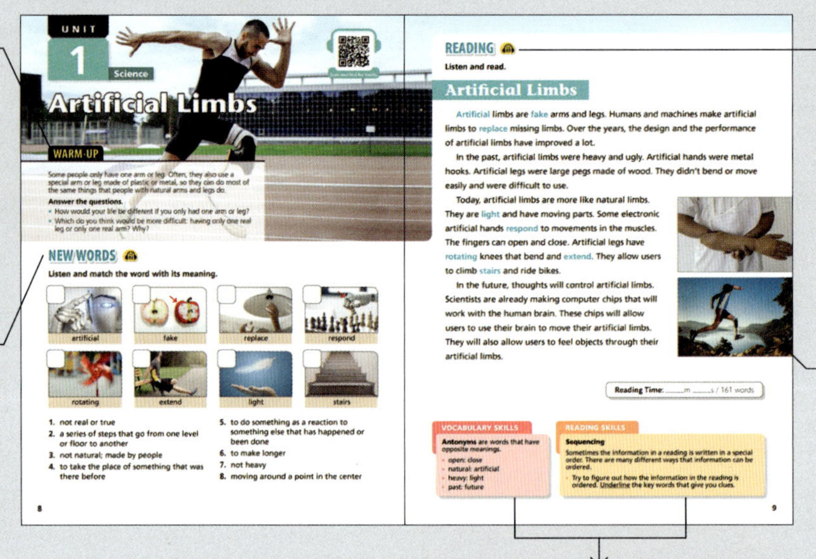

READING

Reading the passage, students learn new information related to school subjects. New words are bolded in the passage.

The images help students understand the text and give more information about the topic.

VOCABULARY SKILLS & READING SKILLS

Vocabulary Skills and Reading Skills enhance students' understanding of the passage.

READING COMPREHENSION

Comprehension questions ensure understanding.

READING SKILLS

Students use different graphic organizers to practice reading skills.

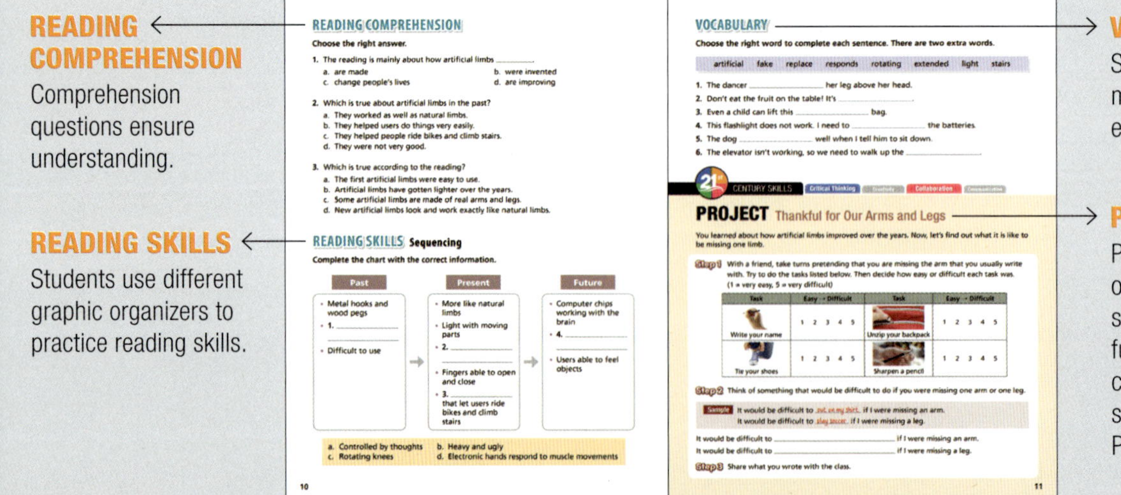

VOCABULARY

Students learn the meaning and use of each word.

PROJECT

Project uses the topic of the unit and allows students to think of further steps. Students can develop 21st century skills through the Project.

Workbook

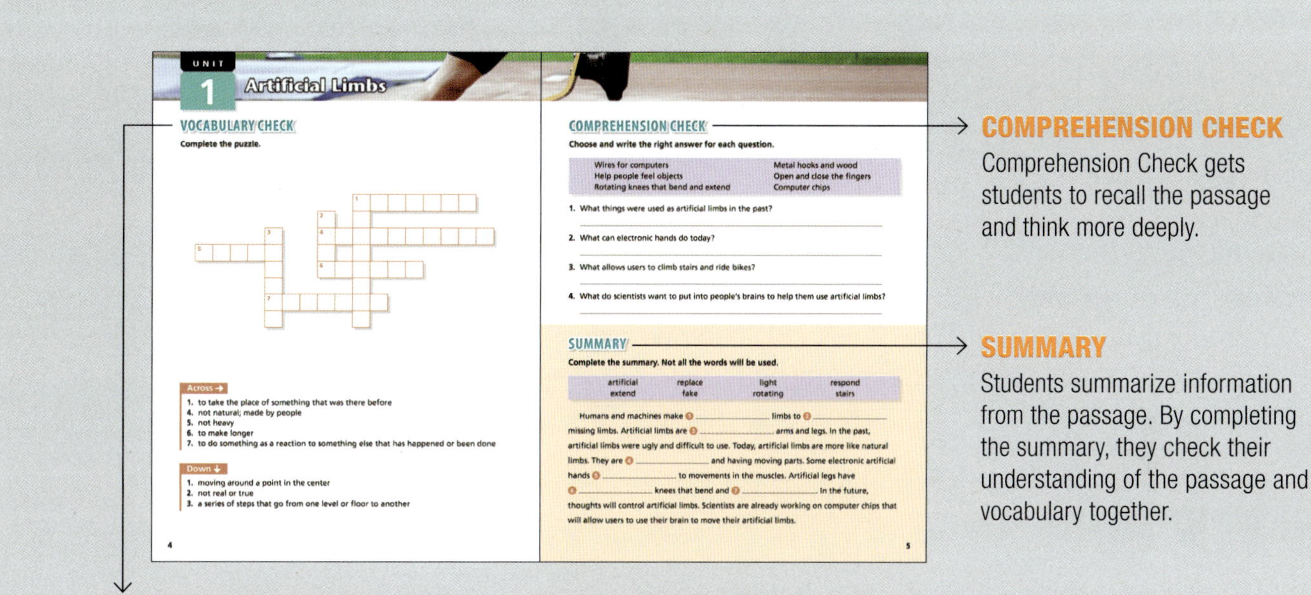

COMPREHENSION CHECK

Comprehension Check gets students to recall the passage and think more deeply.

SUMMARY

Students summarize information from the passage. By completing the summary, they check their understanding of the passage and vocabulary together.

VOCABULARY CHECK

Vocabulary Check gets students to recall the meaning, usage, and spelling of vocabulary.

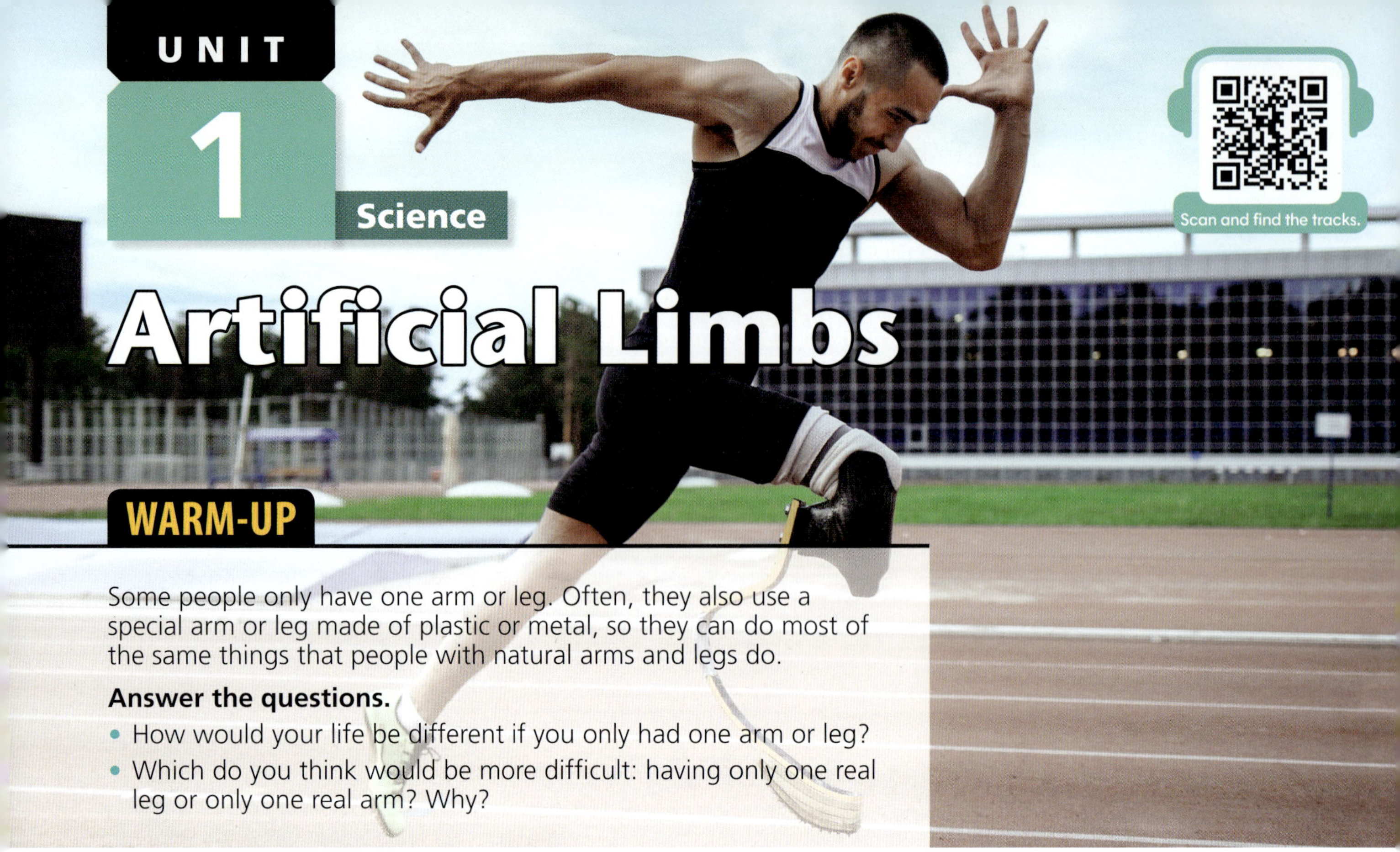

Artificial Limbs

WARM-UP

Some people only have one arm or leg. Often, they also use a special arm or leg made of plastic or metal, so they can do most of the same things that people with natural arms and legs do.

Answer the questions.
- How would your life be different if you only had one arm or leg?
- Which do you think would be more difficult: having only one real leg or only one real arm? Why?

NEW WORDS  Track 02

Listen and match the word with its meaning.

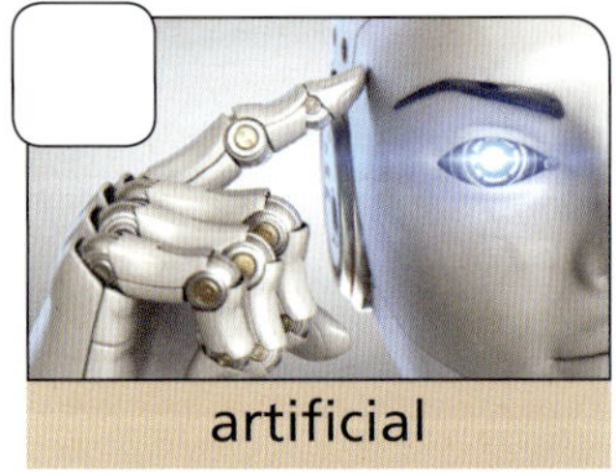
artificial

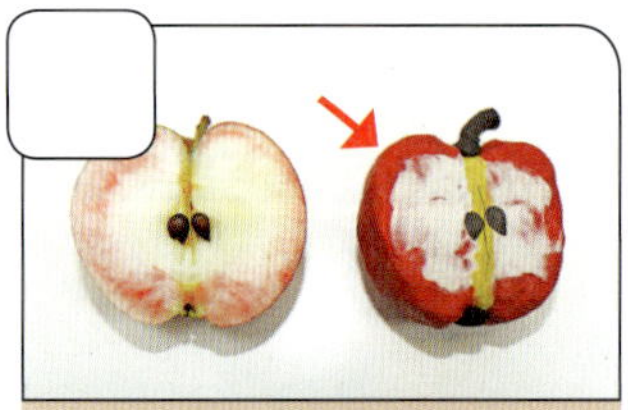

fake

replace

respond

rotating

extend

light

stairs

1. not real or true
2. a series of steps that go from one level or floor to another
3. not natural; made by people
4. to take the place of something that was there before
5. to do something as a reaction to something else that has happened or been done
6. to make longer
7. not heavy
8. moving around a point in the center

Listen and read.

Artificial Limbs

Artificial limbs are fake arms and legs. Humans and machines make artificial limbs to replace missing limbs. Over the years, the design and the performance of artificial limbs have improved a lot.

In the past, artificial limbs were heavy and ugly. Artificial hands were metal hooks. Artificial legs were large pegs made of wood. They didn't bend or move easily and were difficult to use.

Today, artificial limbs are more like natural limbs. They are light and have moving parts. Some electronic artificial hands respond to movements in the muscles. The fingers can open and close. Artificial legs have rotating knees that bend and extend. They allow users to climb stairs and ride bikes.

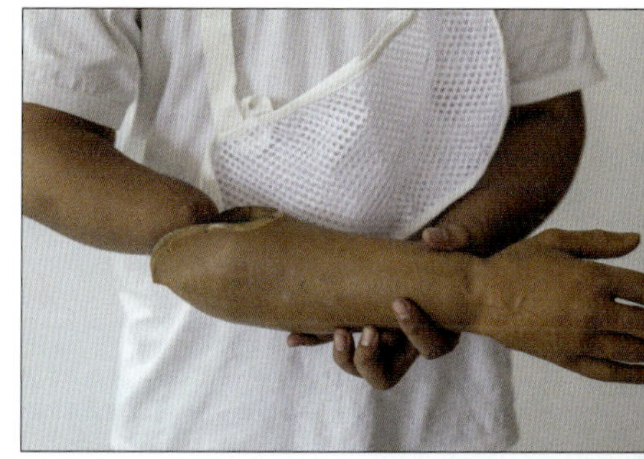

In the future, thoughts will control artificial limbs. Scientists are already making computer chips that will work with the human brain. These chips will allow users to use their brain to move their artificial limbs. They will also allow users to feel objects through their artificial limbs.

Reading Time: _____m _____s / 161 words

VOCABULARY SKILLS

Antonyms are words that have opposite meanings.

- open: close
- natural: artificial
- heavy: light
- past: future

READING SKILLS

Sequencing

Sometimes the information in a reading is written in a special order. There are many different ways that information can be ordered.

- Try to figure out how the information in the reading is ordered. <u>Underline</u> the key words that give you clues.

READING COMPREHENSION

Choose the right answer.

1. The reading is mainly about how artificial limbs __________.

   a. are made
   b. were invented
   c. change people's lives
   d. are improving

2. Which is true about artificial limbs in the past?

   a. They worked as well as natural limbs.
   b. They helped users do things very easily.
   c. They helped people ride bikes and climb stairs.
   d. They were not very good.

3. Which is true according to the reading?

   a. The first artificial limbs were easy to use.
   b. Artificial limbs have gotten lighter over the years.
   c. Some artificial limbs are made of real arms and legs.
   d. New artificial limbs look and work exactly like natural limbs.

READING SKILLS Sequencing

Complete the chart with the correct information.

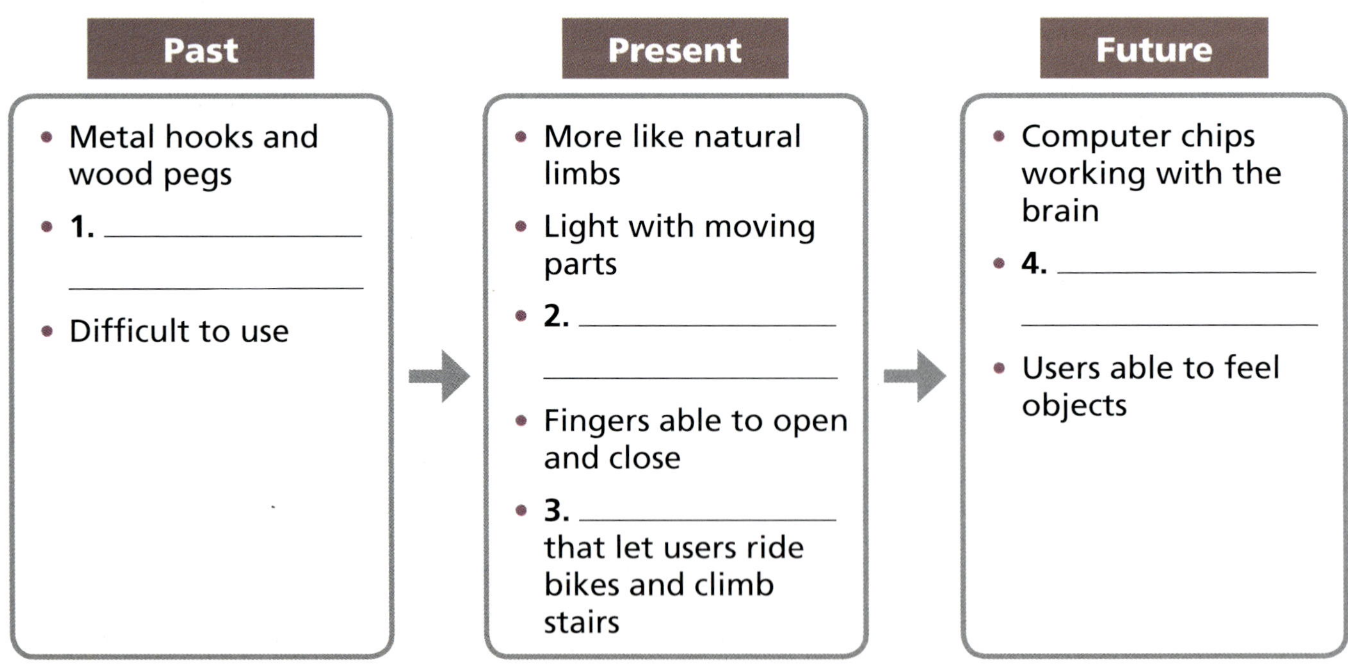

VOCABULARY

Choose the right word to complete each sentence. There are two extra words.

artificial	fake	replace	responds	rotating	extended	light	stairs

1. The dancer _________________ her leg above her head.
2. Don't eat the fruit on the table! It's _________________.
3. Even a child can lift this _________________ bag.
4. This flashlight does not work. I need to _________________ the batteries.
5. The dog _________________ well when I tell him to sit down.
6. The elevator isn't working, so we need to walk up the _________________.

21st CENTURY SKILLS Critical Thinking Creativity Collaboration Communication

PROJECT Thankful for Our Arms and Legs

You learned about how artificial limbs improved over the years. Now, let's find out what it is like to be missing one limb.

Step 1 With a friend, take turns pretending that you are missing the arm that you usually write with. Try to do the tasks listed below. Then decide how easy or difficult each task was. (1 = very easy, 5 = very difficult)

Task	Easy → Difficult	Task	Easy → Difficult
Write your name	1 2 3 4 5	Unzip your backpack	1 2 3 4 5
Tie your shoes	1 2 3 4 5	Sharpen a pencil	1 2 3 4 5

Step 2 Think of something that would be difficult to do if you were missing one arm or one leg.

Sample It would be difficult to _put on my shirt_ if I were missing an arm.
It would be difficult to _play soccer_ if I were missing a leg.

It would be difficult to _________________ if I were missing an arm.
It would be difficult to _________________ if I were missing a leg.

Step 3 Share what you wrote with the class.

UNIT 2

Science

Scan and find the tracks.

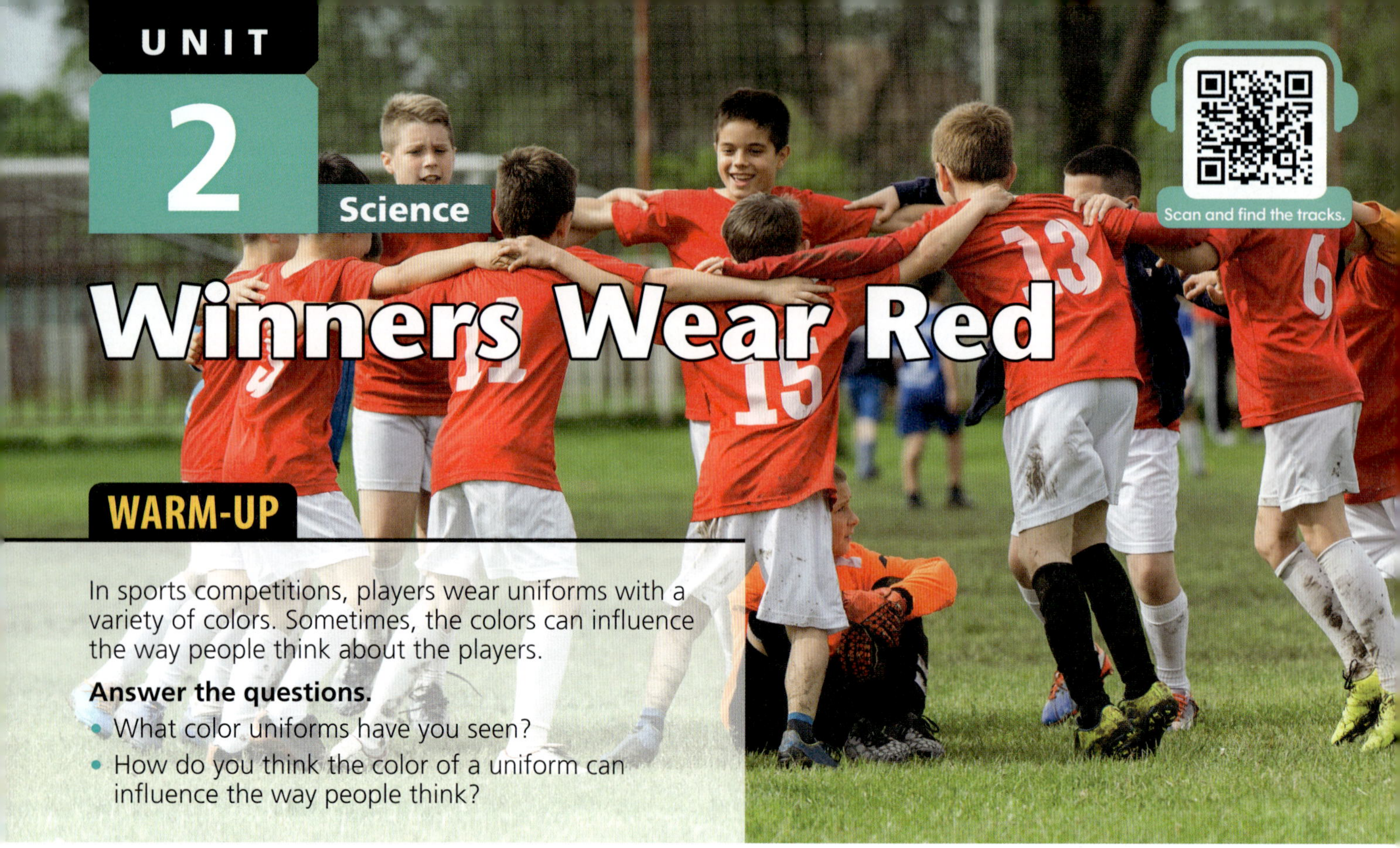

Winners Wear Red

WARM-UP

In sports competitions, players wear uniforms with a variety of colors. Sometimes, the colors can influence the way people think about the players.

Answer the questions.

- What color uniforms have you seen?
- How do you think the color of a uniform can influence the way people think?

NEW WORDS

Track 04

Listen and match the word with its meaning.

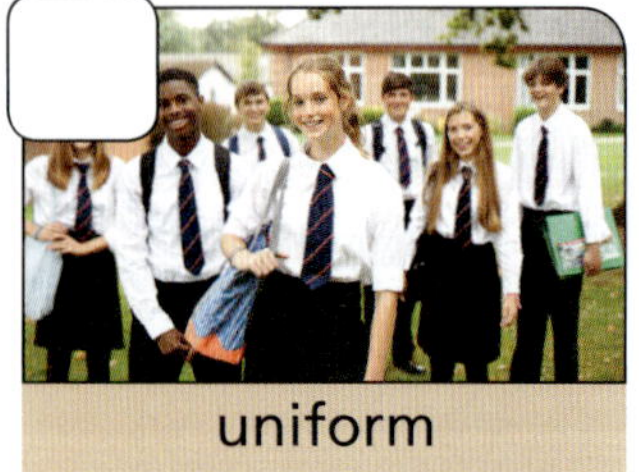

uniform

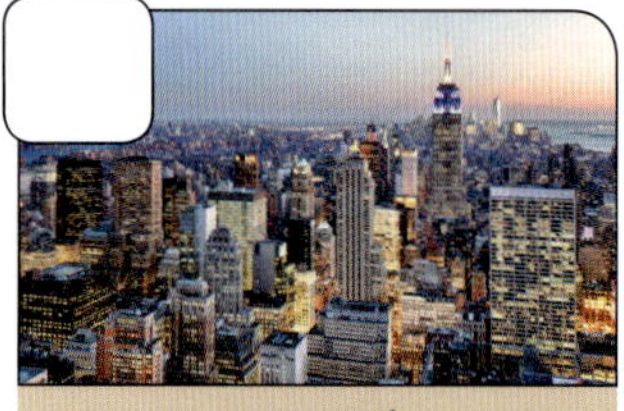

recent

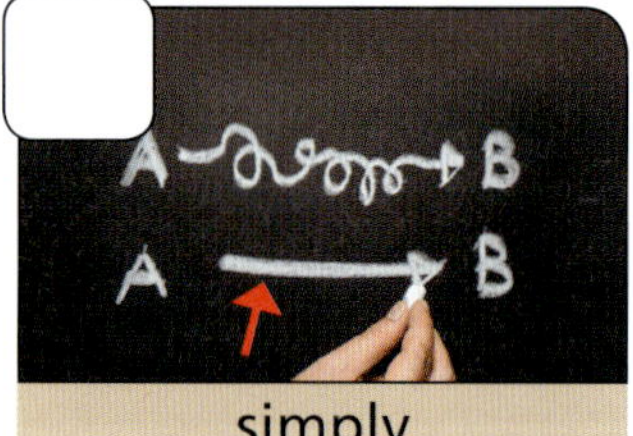

simply

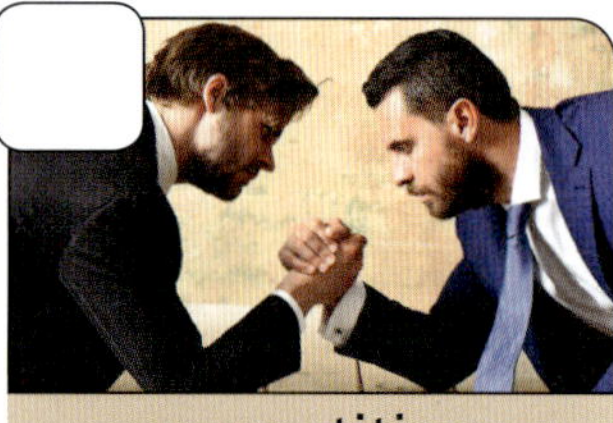

competition

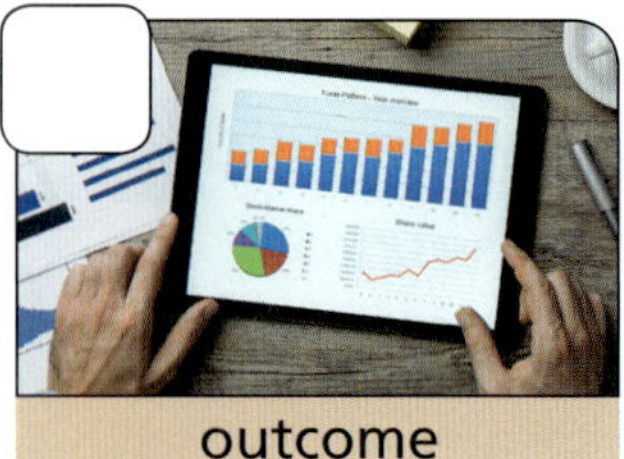

outcome

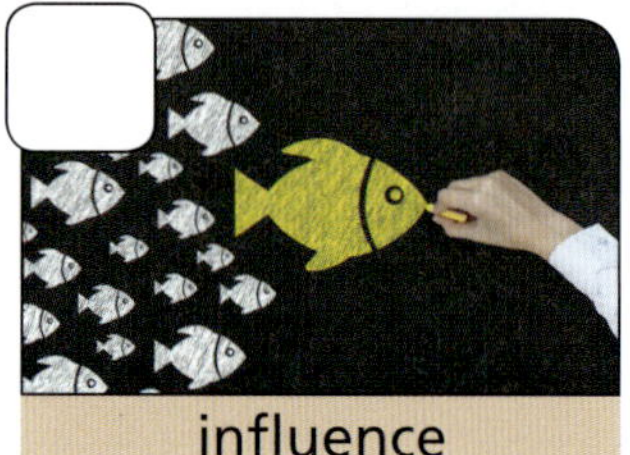

influence

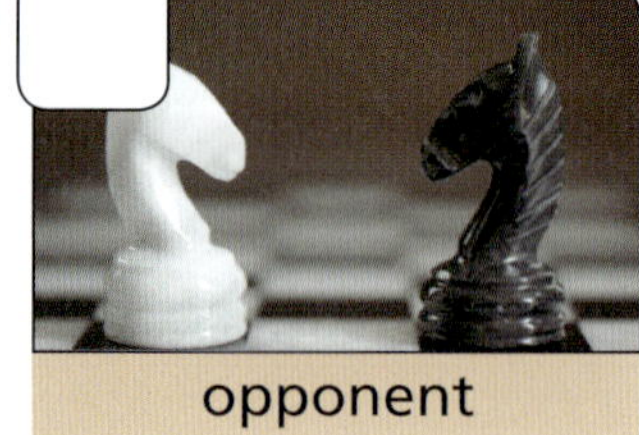

opponent

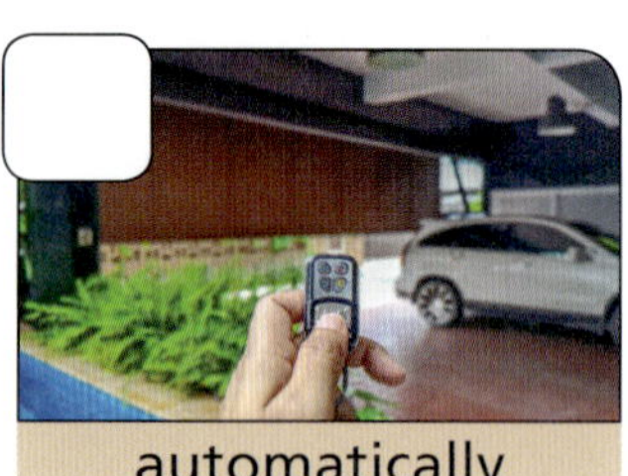

automatically

1. a special kind of clothing that is worn by all the members of a group
2. to have an effect on someone or something
3. happening a short time ago
4. just; only
5. a result
6. in a way that always happens without having to try to make it happen
7. a contest in which people try to win by being better, faster, etc., than others
8. a person or group that you are playing against in a contest

Winners Wear Red

Athletes can choose a **uniform** of any color. Some **simply** choose their favorite color. They don't think about it carefully.

But if you're an athlete, you should try to wear red whenever possible. In a **recent** study, British researchers found that wearing red can help athletes. In fact, athletes who wear red are more likely to win.

The researchers went to some of the largest sports **competitions** in the world. They wanted to know if changing the uniform color would change the **outcome** of a match. They studied many athletes in several different sports. The results showed that wearing red gives an advantage. Athletes who wore red won more <u>matches</u>. They beat their **opponents** who wore other colors.

Of course, you cannot simply put on a red shirt and expect that you will **automatically** win every match. There are other things that **influence** the outcome of a match, too. But the color of the uniform seems to be important.

Reading Time: _____m _____s / 160 words

VOCABULARY SKILLS

The conjunction **if** has two different uses:

- to say one thing can happen only after another happens
  e.g. I'm sorry **if** I've made you angry.

- to show two or more possibilities
  e.g. I don't care **if** he likes it or not.

READING SKILLS

Main Idea & Details

The main idea is the topic of a reading. Details are provided to support and develop the main idea.

- <u>Underline</u> the details that support the main idea of the reading.

READING COMPREHENSION

Choose the right answer.

1. What is the reading mainly about?
- a. Different types of sports competitions
- b. Sports that need uniforms
- c. Colors that athletes wear
- d. Comparing old and new uniforms

2. What does the word <u>matches</u> in line 14 mean in the reading?
- a. Pairs of athletes
- b. Sports competitions
- c. Colors that go together
- d. Research experiments

3. Which is true about the study in the reading?
- a. It found that some athletes wearing red did not win.
- b. Most of the athletes researchers studied wore red.
- c. The athletes were friends with the researchers.
- d. It found that athletes who wore red were stronger.

READING SKILLS Main Idea & Details

Complete the chart with the words in the box.

different	matches	researchers	advantage

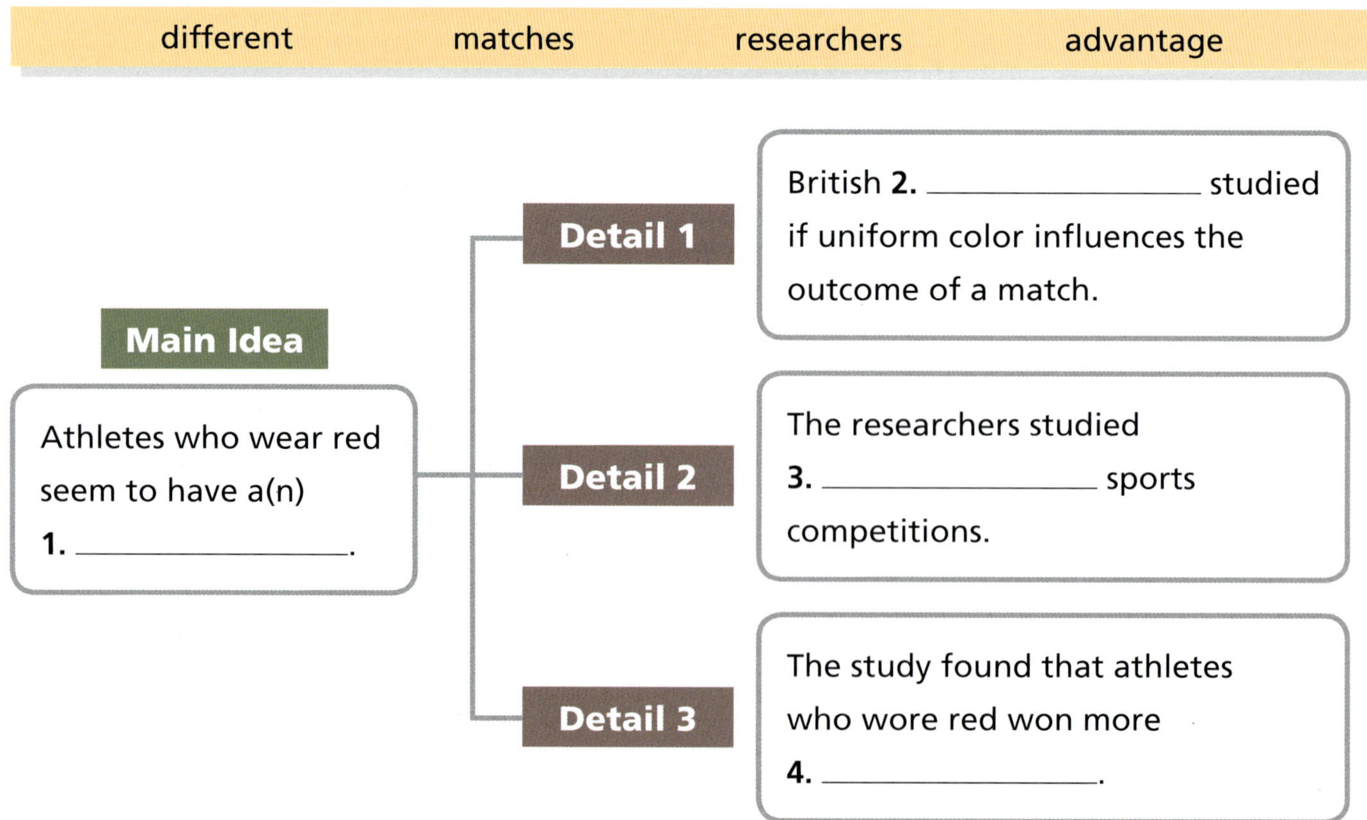

VOCABULARY

Choose the right word to complete each sentence. There are two extra words.

| uniform   outcome   competition   automatically   recent   opponent   influence   simply |

1. I wear my soccer ________________ to the game.

2. The track and field ________________ will last all day and there will be many different matches.

3. Most computers ________________ let you know when a word is spelled incorrectly.

4. TV can ________________ the way children act.

5. You're lucky! The ________________ of your test was very good.

6. This picture is old. Do you have a more ________________ one?

PROJECT Colors and Feelings

You learned that athletes who wear red are more likely to win. Let's talk about other colors and how they make us feel.

Step 1   Think of a color other than red. How does the color make you feel?

Sample   The color _green_ makes me feel _comfortable_.

The color ________________ makes me feel ________________.

Step 2   Ask your friends how the color you chose makes them feel. Share your answers with the class.

Name	Feeling

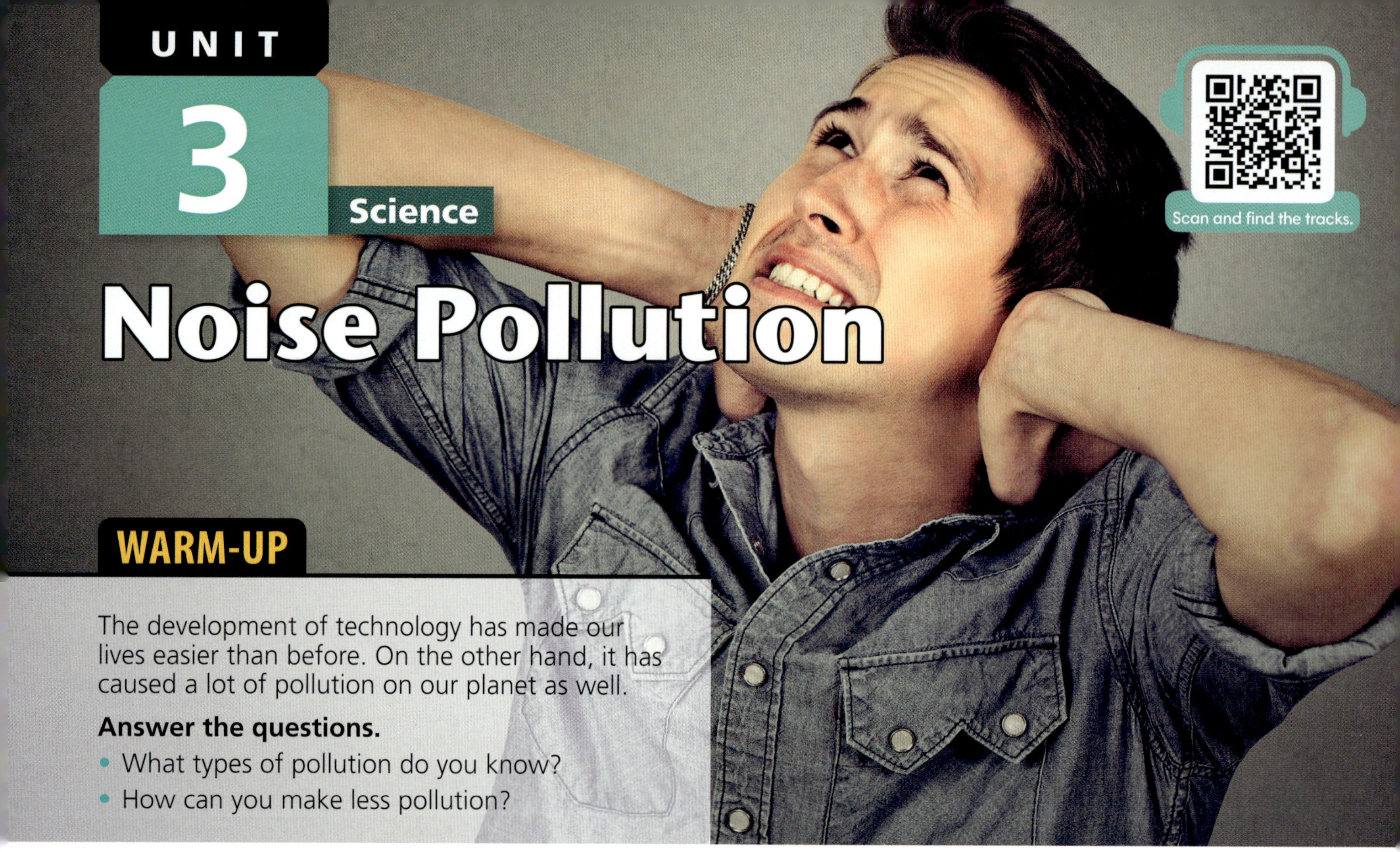

UNIT 3 Science

Noise Pollution

Scan and find the tracks.

WARM-UP

The development of technology has made our lives easier than before. On the other hand, it has caused a lot of pollution on our planet as well.

Answer the questions.

- What types of pollution do you know?
- How can you make less pollution?

NEW WORDS

Track 06

Listen and match the word with its meaning.

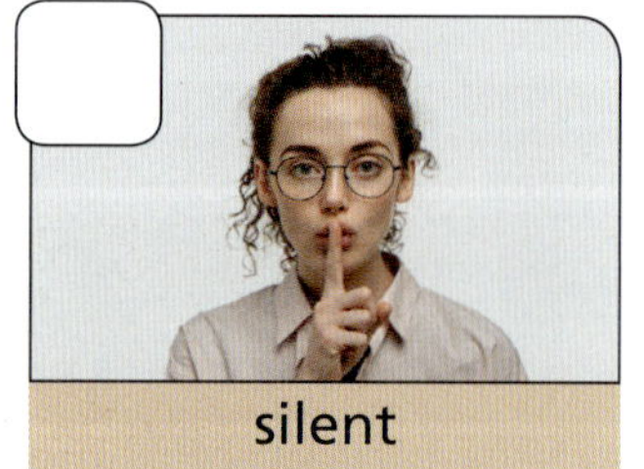

silent

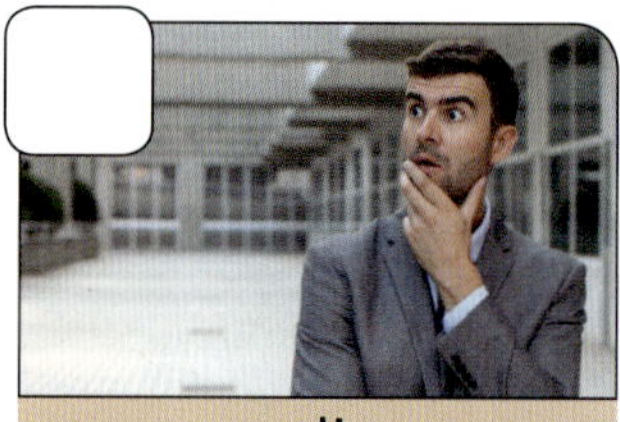

realize

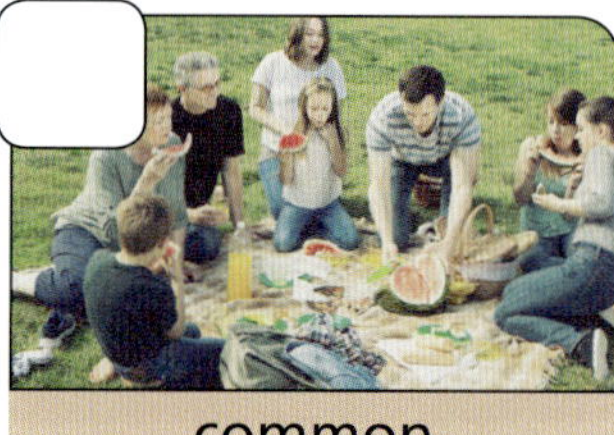

common

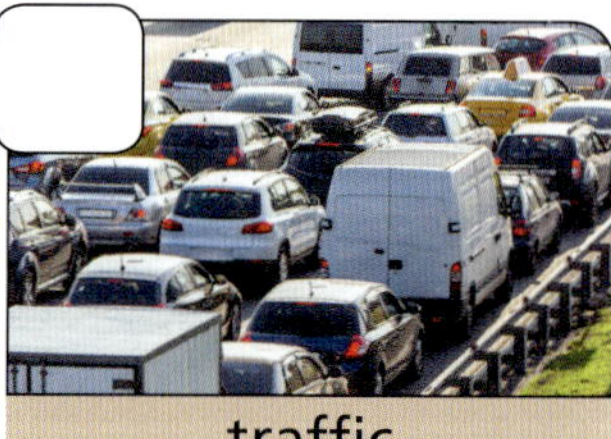

traffic

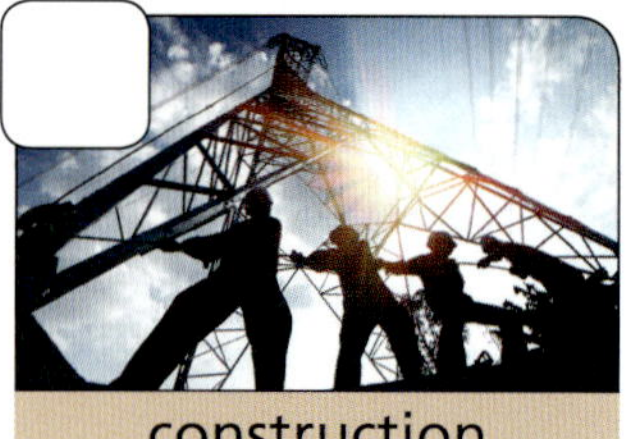

construction

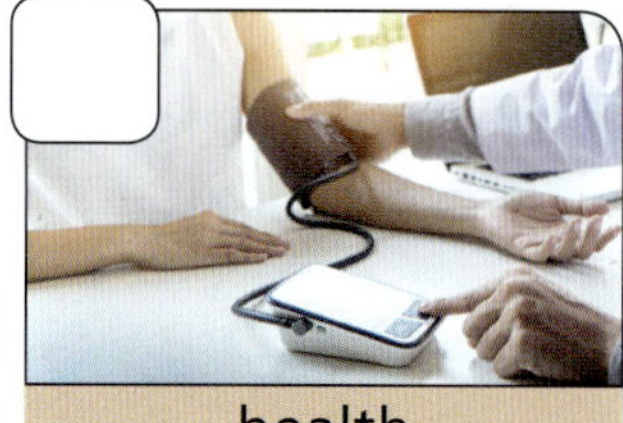

health

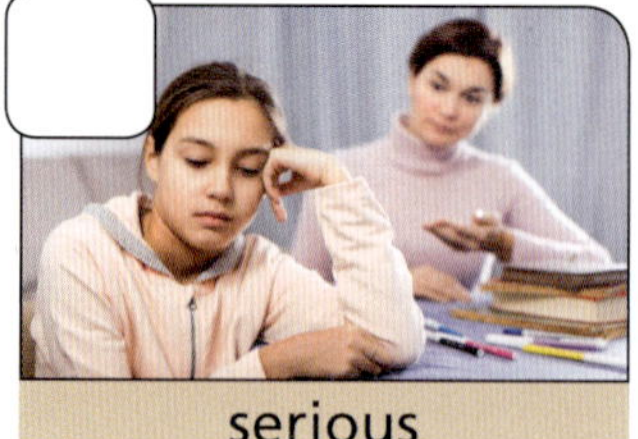

serious

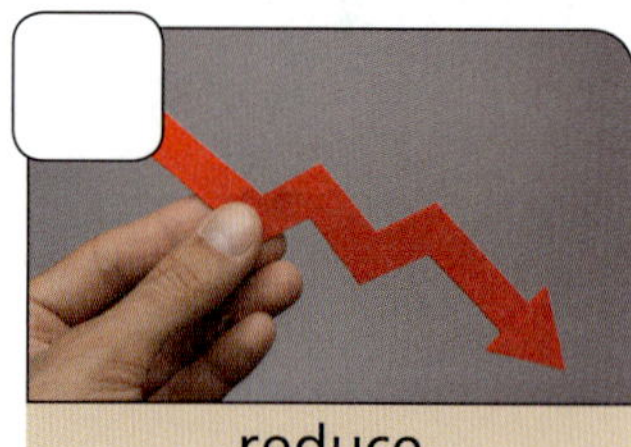

reduce

1. being important or possibly dangerous
2. the building of things like houses
3. to make something smaller or less
4. done by many people; usual
5. all the cars, trucks, etc., driving on a road
6. the condition of the body
7. without sound
8. to learn; to understand

READING

Listen and read.

Noise Pollution

Most people think their home is silent when everyone is sleeping. But maybe there is a little noise from the fridge. Or maybe there is the sound of cars from a nearby road. You may not realize it, but this noise is a form of pollution.

If you ask people about the problem of pollution, many people respond by talking about air or water pollution. But one of the most common forms of pollution is noise pollution. This is human- or machine-made sound that has a bad effect on human health. Most noise pollution comes from traffic. However, planes, construction, or even loud TVs add to the problem.

Noise pollution affects our health. It can cause hearing problems and stress. Over time, stress can cause other serious problems in our bodies. People should try to reduce the noise they make. For example, lower the volume on your TV. By reducing our own noise, we can improve our own health and those we live with.

Reading Time: _____m _____s / 164 words

VOCABULARY SKILLS

The suffix **-tion** creates nouns out of verbs.

construct+tion → construc**tion**

- informa**tion**: facts, data, details, and knowledge about things
- ac**tion**: what someone does
- solu**tion**: a way of fixing a problem

READING SKILLS

Reviewing

In a reading, the definition of a new word is often followed by supporting details and examples.

- Circle one new term and its definition in the reading.
- Underline the example(s) after it.

READING COMPREHENSION

Choose the right answer.

1. What is the reading mainly about?
   a. Noise that affects health
   b. Noises that make people angry
   c. Silent places
   d. Natural sounds that are scary

2. Noise from _________ is NOT mentioned in the reading.
   a. cars
   b. children
   c. jets
   d. TVs

3. What advice does the writer give in the reading?
   a. Do not buy large TVs.
   b. Do not live in big cities.
   c. Try not to drive cars.
   d. Try to cut down our own noise.

READING SKILLS Reviewing

Complete the chart with the words and phrase in the box.

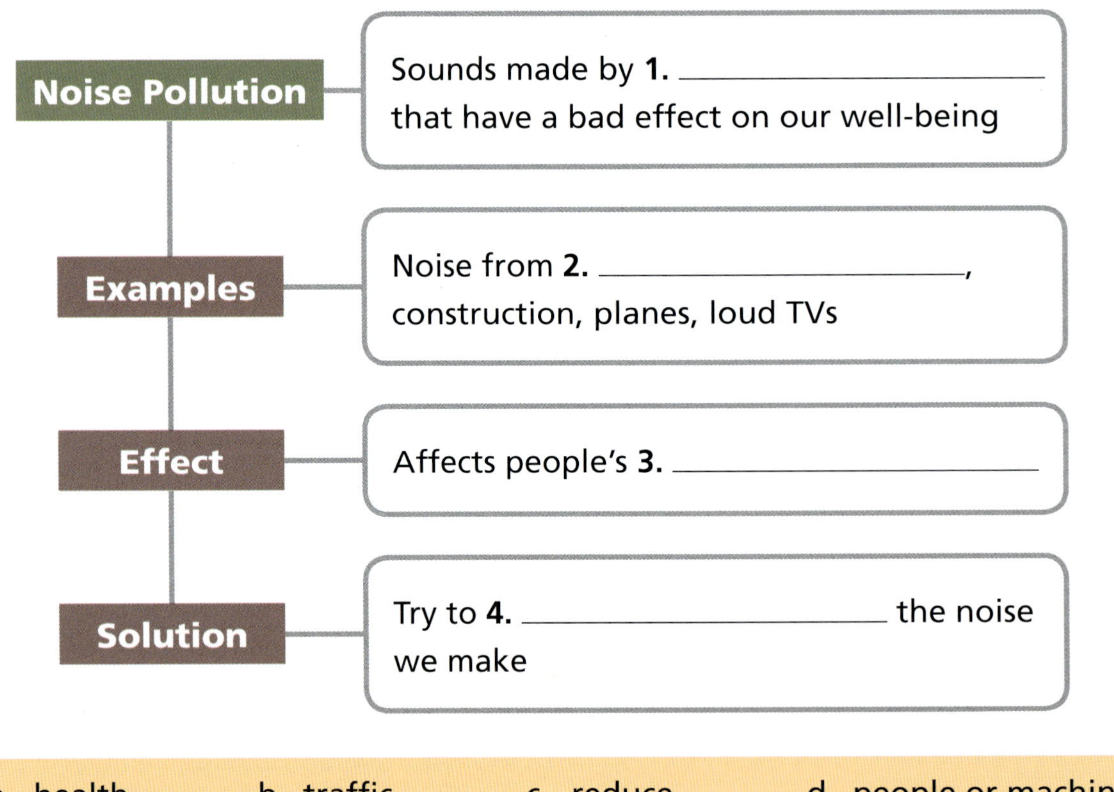

a. health   b. traffic   c. reduce   d. people or machines

VOCABULARY

Choose the right word to complete each sentence. There are two extra words.

| traffic | silent | serious | realize | common | construction | health | reduce |

1. I didn't _________________ we lived near each other.

2. We need to exercise more often for our _________________.

3. Let's leave early, before the _________________ gets bad.

4. We should _________________ the time we spend watching TV.

5. The classroom was empty and _________________.

6. The road is closed because of _________________.

21st CENTURY SKILLS

Critical Thinking Creativity Collaboration Communication

PROJECT Quiet Places

You learned that noise pollution is not good for our health. Let's talk about quiet places where we can go to relax.

Step 1 Think about quiet places. Which quiet place would you like to go to? Why?

Sample _The forest_ is a quiet place I would like to go to because _I can relax and enjoy nature there_.

_________________ is a quiet place I would like to go to because

____.

Step 2 Think about why quiet places are or are not important and why.

Sample Quiet places (are / are not) important because _we can relax without being bothered_.

Quiet places (are / are not) important because _________________

____.

UNIT

4 Science

Understanding the Heart

Scan and find the tracks.

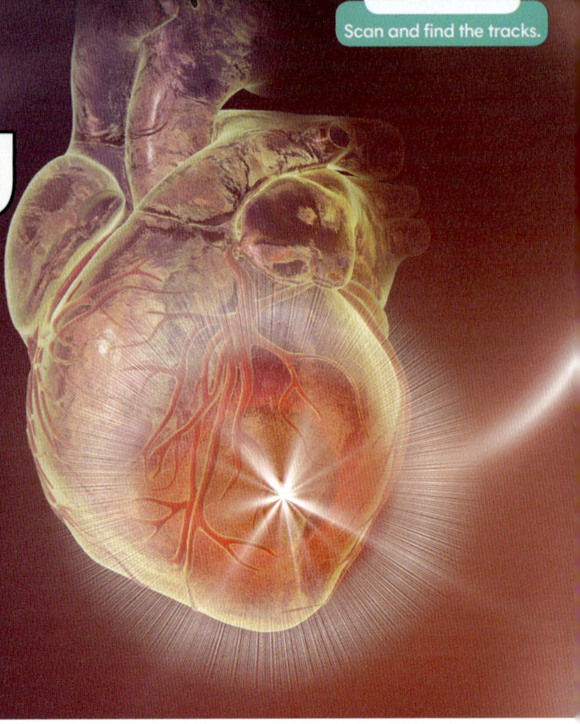

WARM-UP

The heart is one of the most important organs in a human's body. It helps other organs work properly.

Answer the questions.

- Where is your heart in your body?
- How does the heart help other organs?

NEW WORDS

Track 08

Listen and match the word with its meaning.

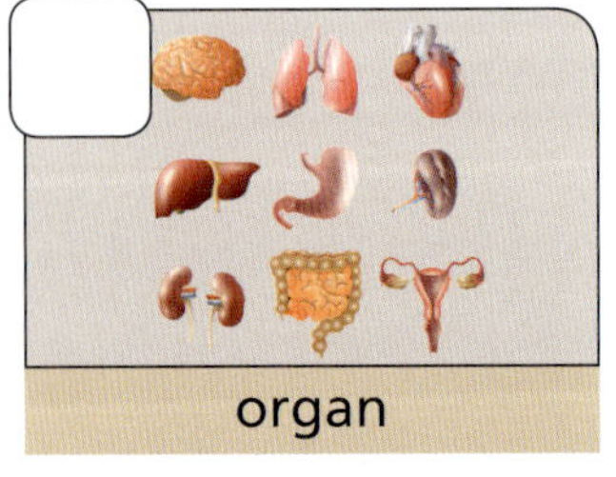

organ

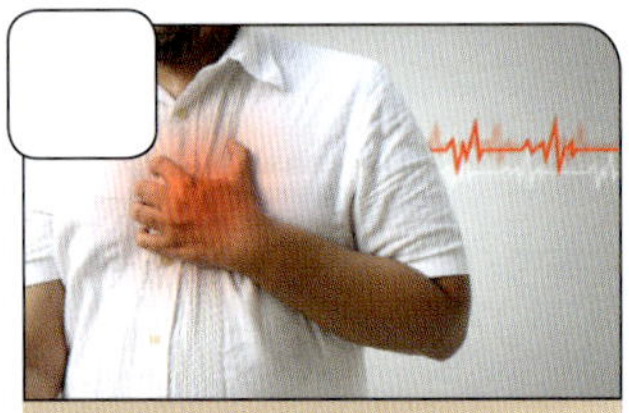

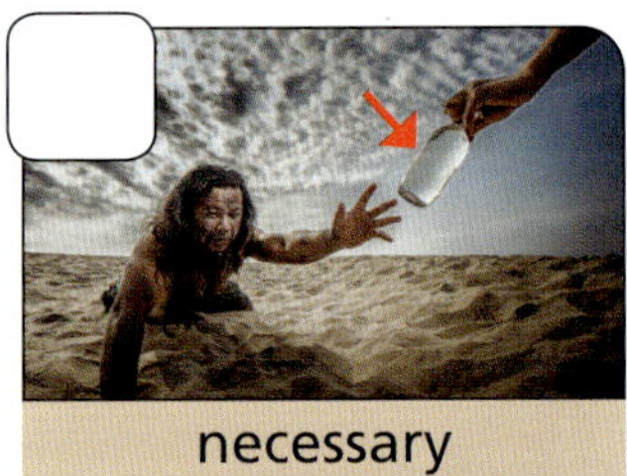

vital

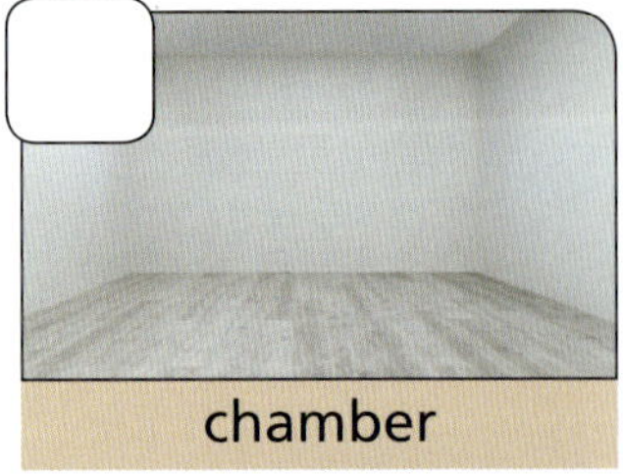

necessary

chamber

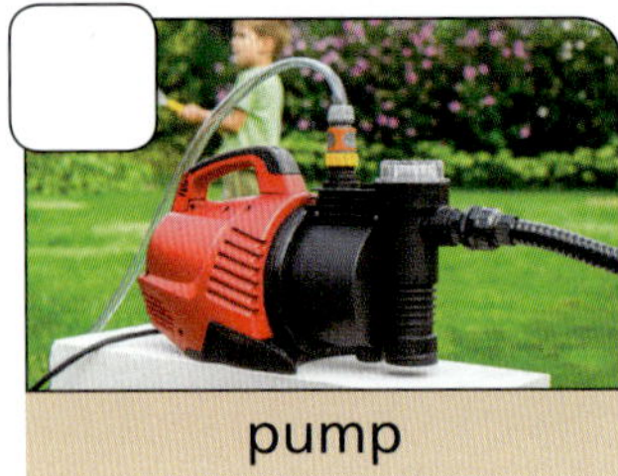

pump

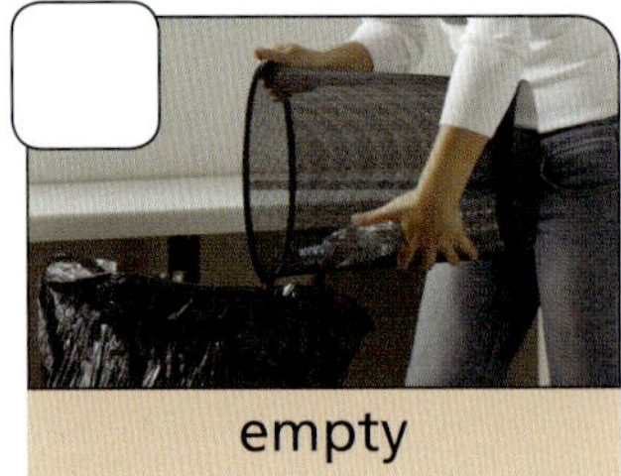

empty

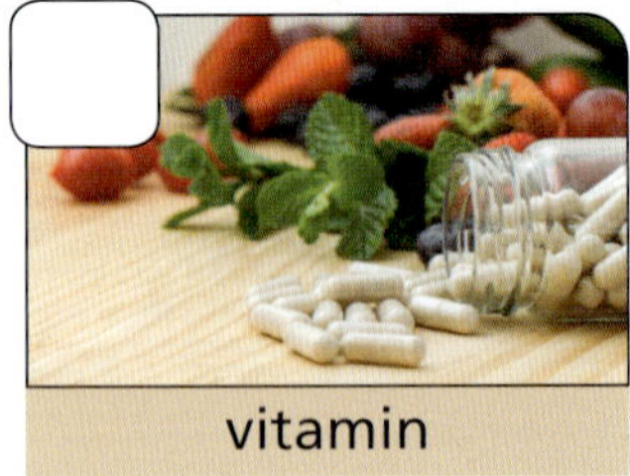

vitamin

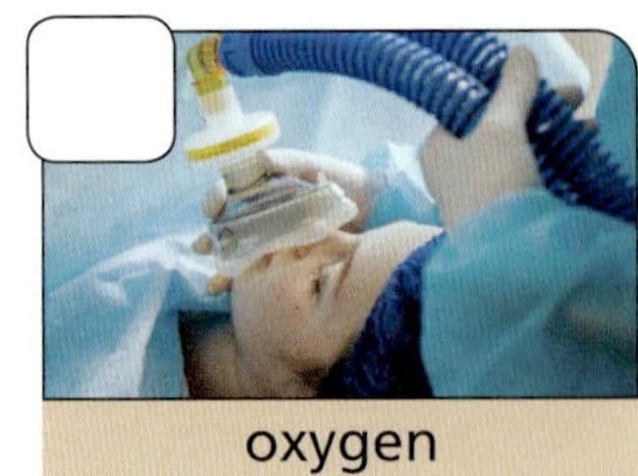

oxygen

1. to make liquid or gas flow
2. a natural thing that is usually in food and that helps your body to be healthy
3. so important that you must do it or have it; absolutely needed
4. to remove all of something from something else
5. an important part inside your body
6. a closed space inside something
7. a chemical that is found in the air, that has no color, taste, or smell, and that is needed for life
8. needed to stay alive or for something to be done

Understanding the Heart

The heart is one of the five **vital organs** in the human body. These organs are **necessary** for humans to stay alive. So it's important to understand how the heart works.

Inside the heart, there are four parts called **chambers**. The heart beats and fills the chambers with blood. Then the heart **empties** the chambers. It **pumps** blood from the chambers through the body.

Blood is carried through the body in tubes called vessels. Vessels that carry blood away from the heart are arteries. Vessels that carry blood back to the heart are veins. Blood carries many important things through the body. It carries **vitamins**, **oxygen**, and other important things. It's like a transportation system in the body. If your blood vessels were connected end to end, they would wrap around the Earth twice!

The human heart beats about seventy times per minute. That's 4,200 times per hour! It pumps 7,500 liters of blood through your body every day. It works amazingly hard. So keep your heart healthy!

Reading Time: _____ m _____ s / 168 words

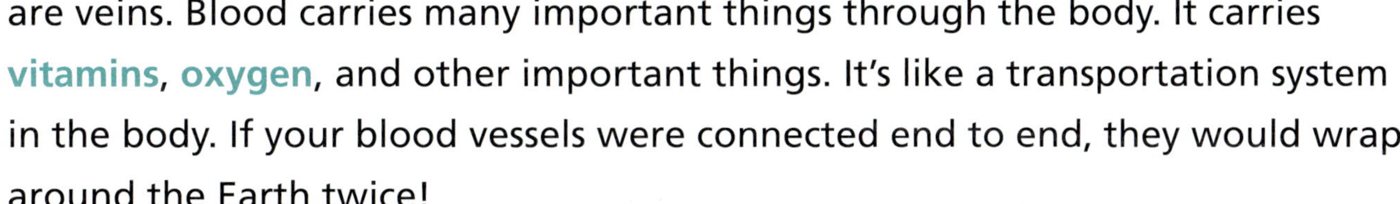

keep+A+B: to cause A (someone or something) to continue as B (state or condition)

So **keep** your heart healthy!
- The TV **keeps** the children quiet.
- Karen wants to **keep** her money safe.
- The sound **keeps** him awake.

Sequencing

Sequencing means the order that things happen. It helps us understand information to know the sequence of events.
- How is blood carried through the body in vessels? <u>Underline</u> the sentences in the reading.

READING COMPREHENSION

Choose the right answer.

1. What is the reading mainly about?
   a. The organs of the body
   b. How the heart works
   c. Your blood vessels
   d. How often the heart beats

2. Which carries blood around the body?
   a. Chambers
   b. Organs
   c. The heart
   d. Vessels

3. Which is true according to the reading?
   a. You can live without your heart.
   b. The heart beats about 4,000 times a day.
   c. There are four different parts in the heart.
   d. Blood carries water through the human body.

READING SKILLS Sequencing

Complete the chart with the words in the box.

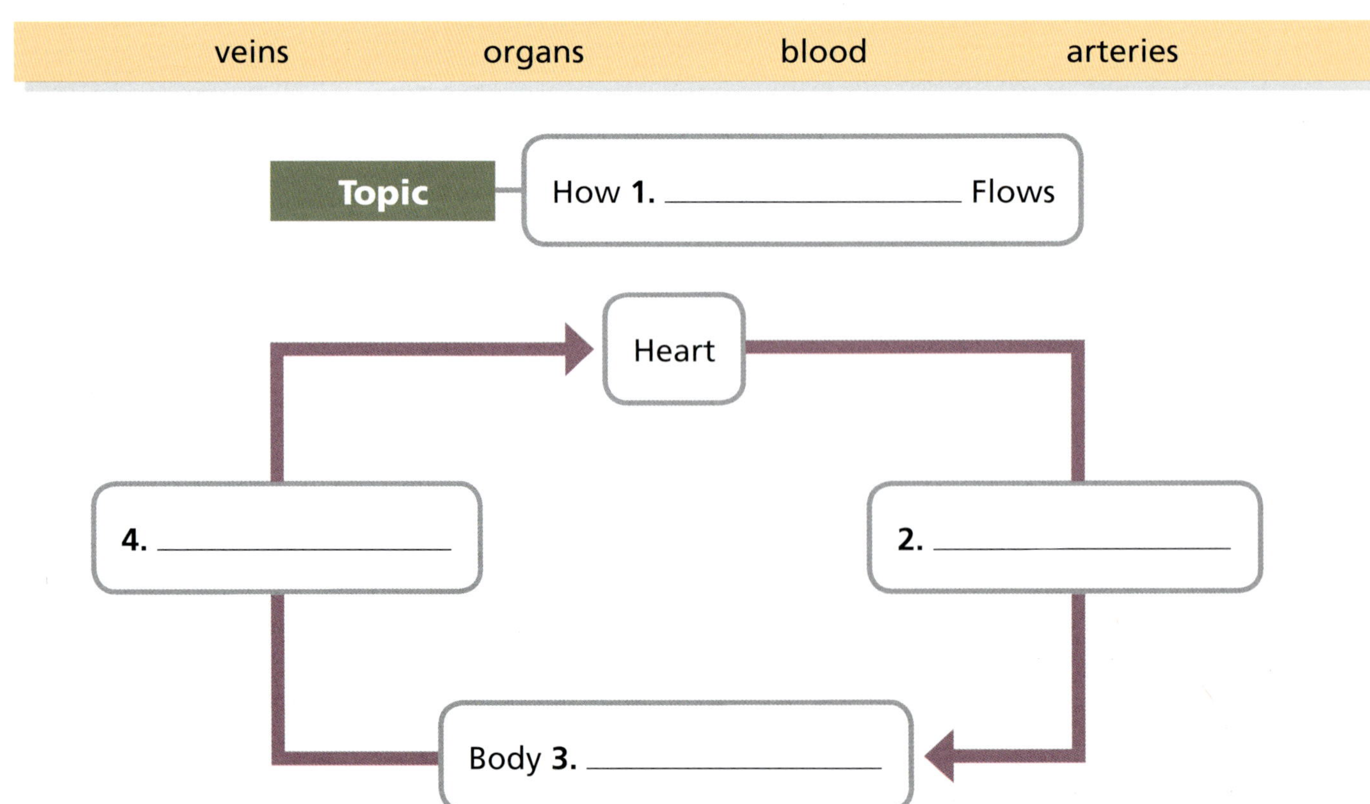

VOCABULARY

Choose the right word to complete each sentence. There are two extra words.

| pumped | vital | organs | empty | necessary | chamber | vitamins | oxygen |

1. I _______________ my backpack when I get home from school by taking all the books out of it.
2. Fish breathe _______________ from the water, but humans breathe it from the air.
3. If you want to do well in school, it is _______________ to listen in class and study hard.
4. Did you know about the secret _______________ under the ground?
5. Eddie _______________ air into the tire of his bike.
6. Fruits and vegetables have lots of _______________ in them that are good for us.

21st CENTURY SKILLS

Critical Thinking Creativity Collaboration Communication

PROJECT A Healthy Heart

You learned that the heart is an amazing organ that pumps blood through your body. Now, let's think about how we can keep our hearts healthy!

Step 1 Think about things we can do to keep our heart healthy. Use the pictures to help you.

1. Eat good food. _______________
2. _______________
3. _______________

Step 2 Decide what you will do to keep your heart healthy. Make a plan for next week. Compare your plan with your friends.

Monday	Tuesday	Wednesday	Thursday	Friday	Saturday	Sunday

UNIT 5

Literature

Scan and find the tracks.

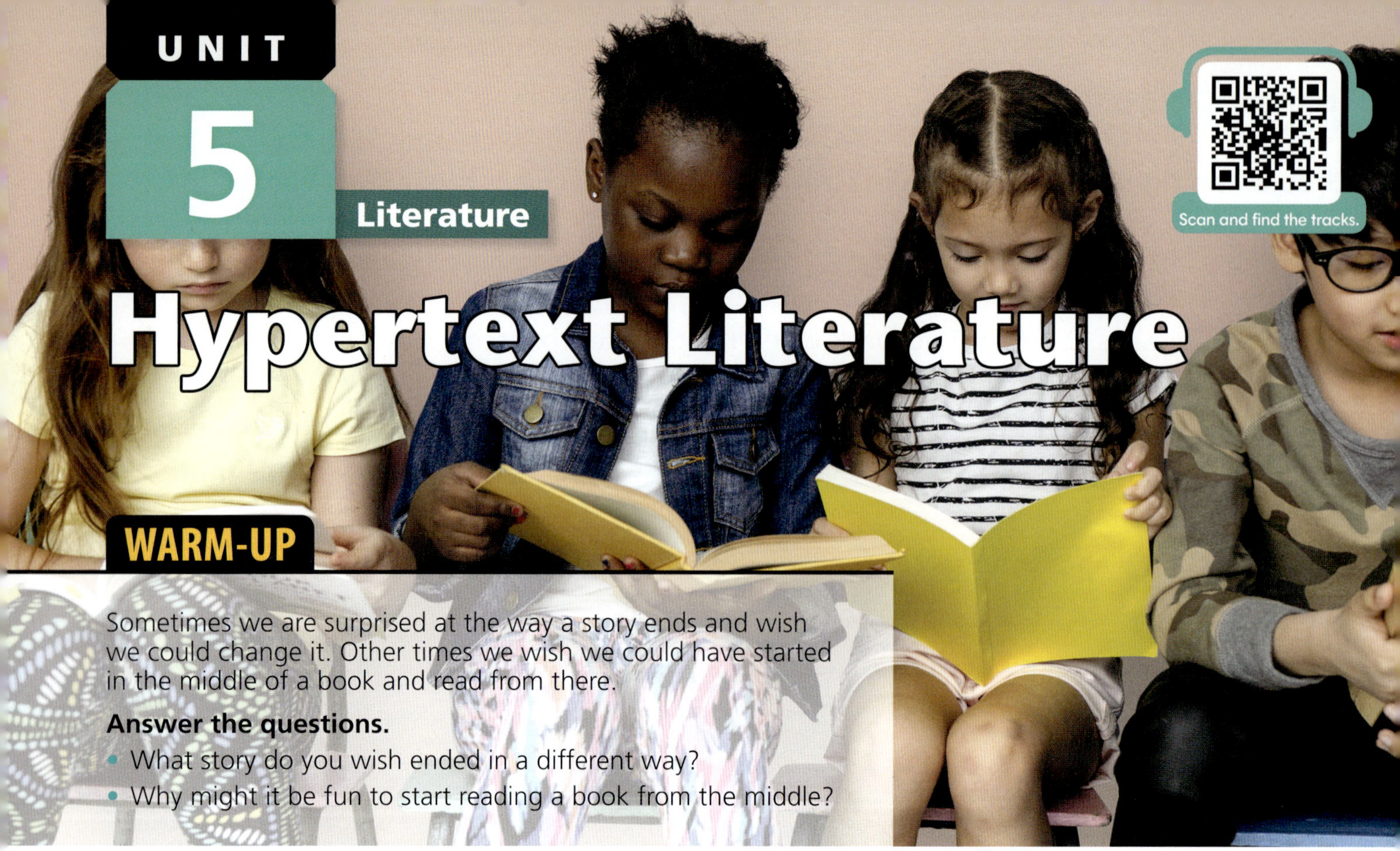

Hypertext Literature

WARM-UP

Sometimes we are surprised at the way a story ends and wish we could change it. Other times we wish we could have started in the middle of a book and read from there.

Answer the questions.

- What story do you wish ended in a different way?
- Why might it be fun to start reading a book from the middle?

NEW WORDS

Track 10

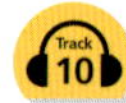

Listen and match the word with its meaning.

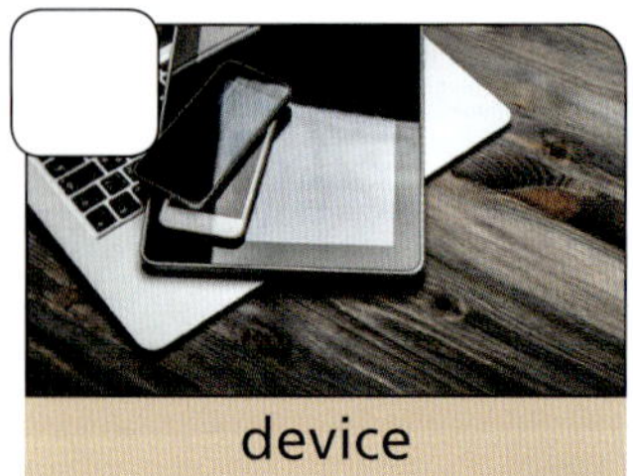

device

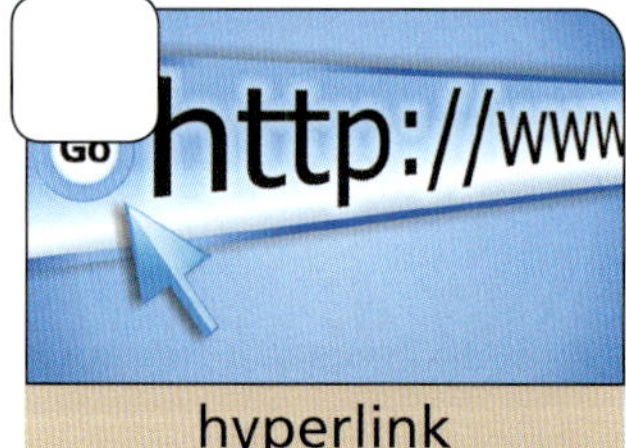

hyperlink

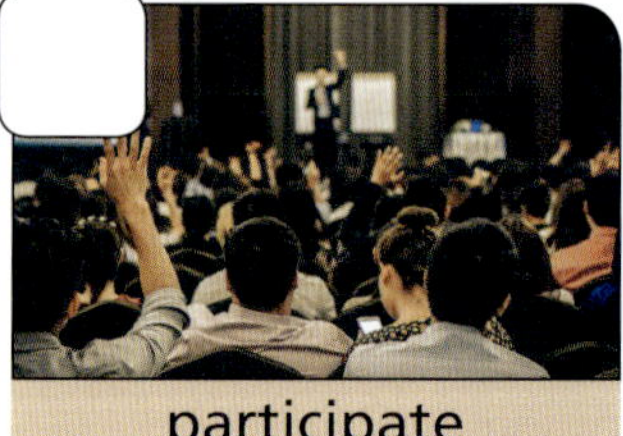

participate

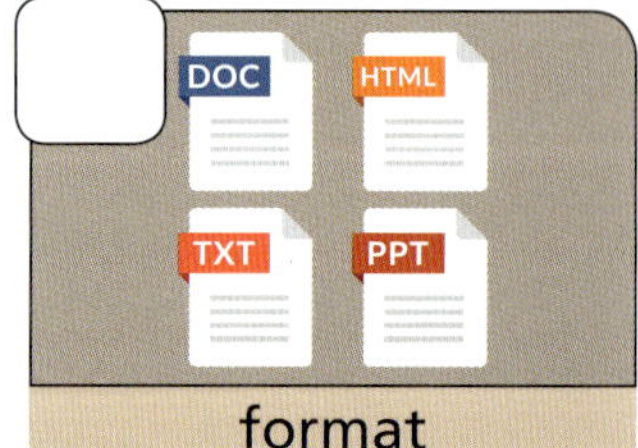

format

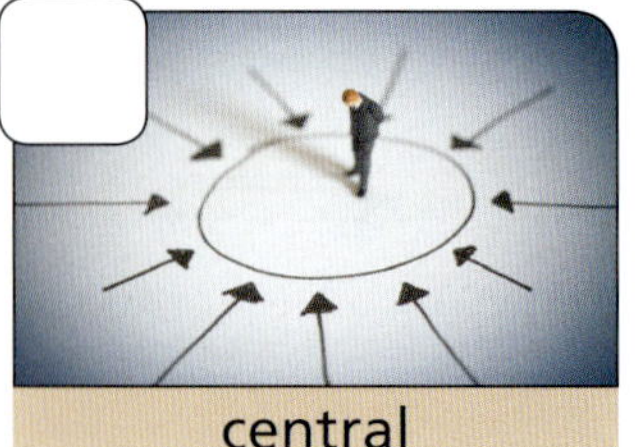

central

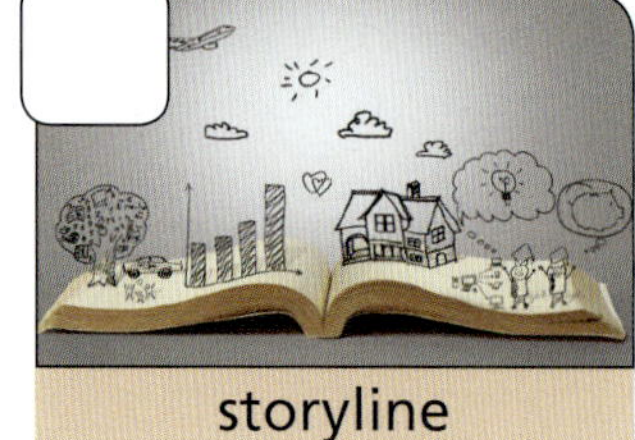

storyline

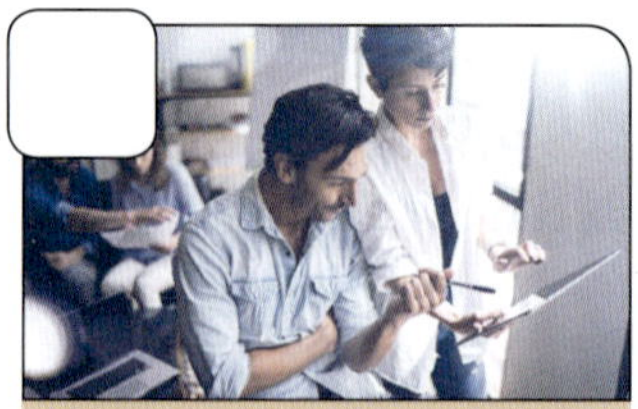

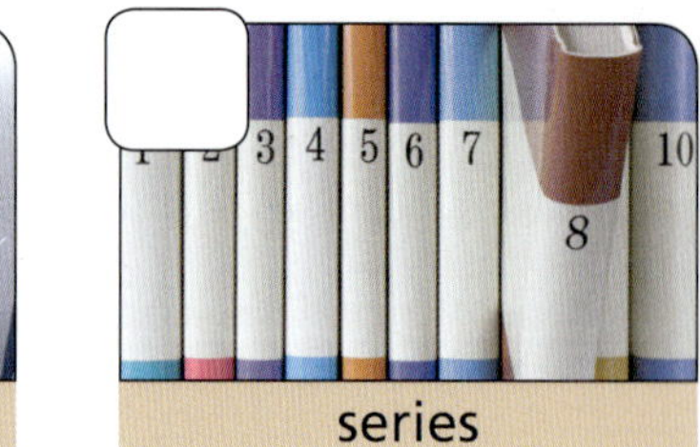

interact

series

1. a machine that is made to be used for some special purpose
2. to do things together with another person or thing
3. a number of things that come one after the other
4. at the center; being the most important part of something
5. to take part in doing an activity
6. the plot of a story
7. a link that takes you to a web page when you click it
8. the way something is organized

Listen and read.

Hypertext Literature

Hypertext literature is a fun way to enjoy stories and books. Using electronic **devices**, readers can **interact** with **hyperlinks** in a story. Instead of reading a story from start to finish, readers **participate** throughout the story. After reading a few pages, readers are given some choices. They need to choose what the characters should do in the story. Readers decide and then click on a hyperlink.

Stories can be put together in different **formats** using hypertext literature. One type has a **central storyline**. Links allow the story to go different ways. Readers eventually return to the main storyline. Another format has links that can change big parts of the story. There is more than one ending. Hypertext literature can also be a mix of formats.

Pottermore is J. K. Rowling's hypertext novel. It is part of the *Harry Potter* **series**. Readers can link to information about the characters. The links help

readers understand more about the other *Harry Potter* books. Hypertext can be an exciting way to experience literature.

> **Reading Time:** _____m _____s / 169 words

VOCABULARY SKILLS

Some words are the same in both the singular and plural form.

series

- **fish**: an animal that lives in water and has a tail and scales
- **sheep**: a farm animal with thick wool
- **deer**: a large wild animal with four legs that eats grass and leaves

READING SKILLS

Classifying

Classifying means putting things into groups that are related or have the same thing in common.

- Underline the type of literature the reading is talking about.

READING COMPREHENSION

Choose the right answer.

1. What is the reading mainly about?
   a. J. K. Rowling's books
   b. How to change a story
   c. A fun type of literature
   d. Characters that make up a story

2. What makes hypertext literature different?
   a. New writers
   b. Links in the text
   c. One ending
   d. Exciting characters

3. Which is NOT true according to the reading?
   a. All hypertext stories have more than one ending.
   b. You can read hyperlink literature now.
   c. Popular writers are making hypertext stories.
   d. Hypertext stories are read on a computer or tablet.

READING SKILLS Classifying

Complete the chart with the correct information.

a. Tell a story

c. Can interact with links

e. May have more than one storyline

b. Read on paper

d. May have more than one ending

f. Read only from start to finish

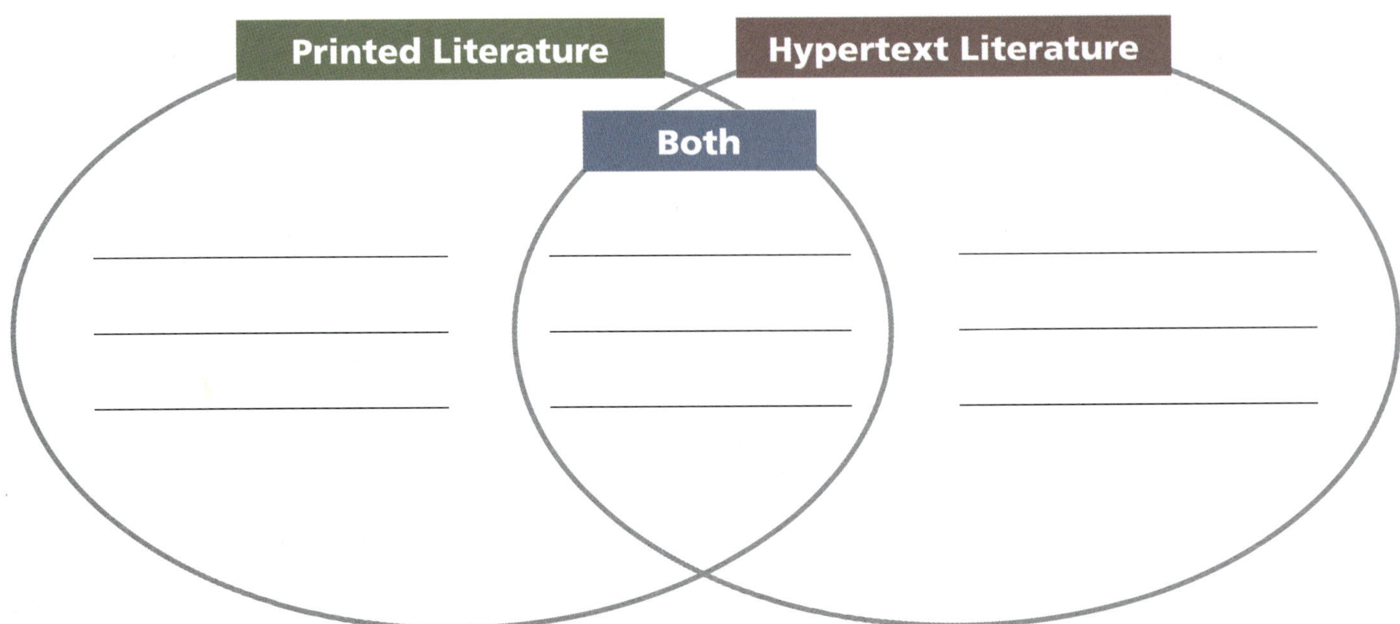

26

VOCABULARY

Choose the right word to complete each sentence. There are two extra words.

| hyperlink | storyline | device | interact | format | central | series | participate |

1. If you click on that _________________, you will open a new page.

2. He did not want to _________________ in the soccer game because he had hurt his leg.

3. The _________________ idea of the reading is that dinosaurs were huge.

4. This book is part of a new _________________ by my favorite writer.

5. Use a picture _________________ to present the information.

6. His _________________ died because he forgot to charge the battery.

PROJECT Make Your Own Story!

You read about hypertext literature. Now, let's create a story with different endings.

Step 1 Work in a group of four. Read the beginning of the story.

> Kim had a problem. She was invited to her friend's party. She did not want to go. The party was at a bowling alley. Kim did not know how to bowl. She did not want her friends to know.
>
> Kim called her friend to tell her she could not go to the party. She did not tell her why. Her friend was sad to hear that Kim was not going. "Please, Kim," she said. "I really want you there."

Step 2 Work together to write a short paragraph on a piece of paper telling what happens next in the story.

| **Sample** | "I don't know how to bowl!" Kim finally said. |

Her friend laughed and said, "None of us know how to bowl! We can all learn together. Come on!"

Kim laughed. "Wow, that sounds like my kind of party!"

Step 3 Present your group's story to the class.

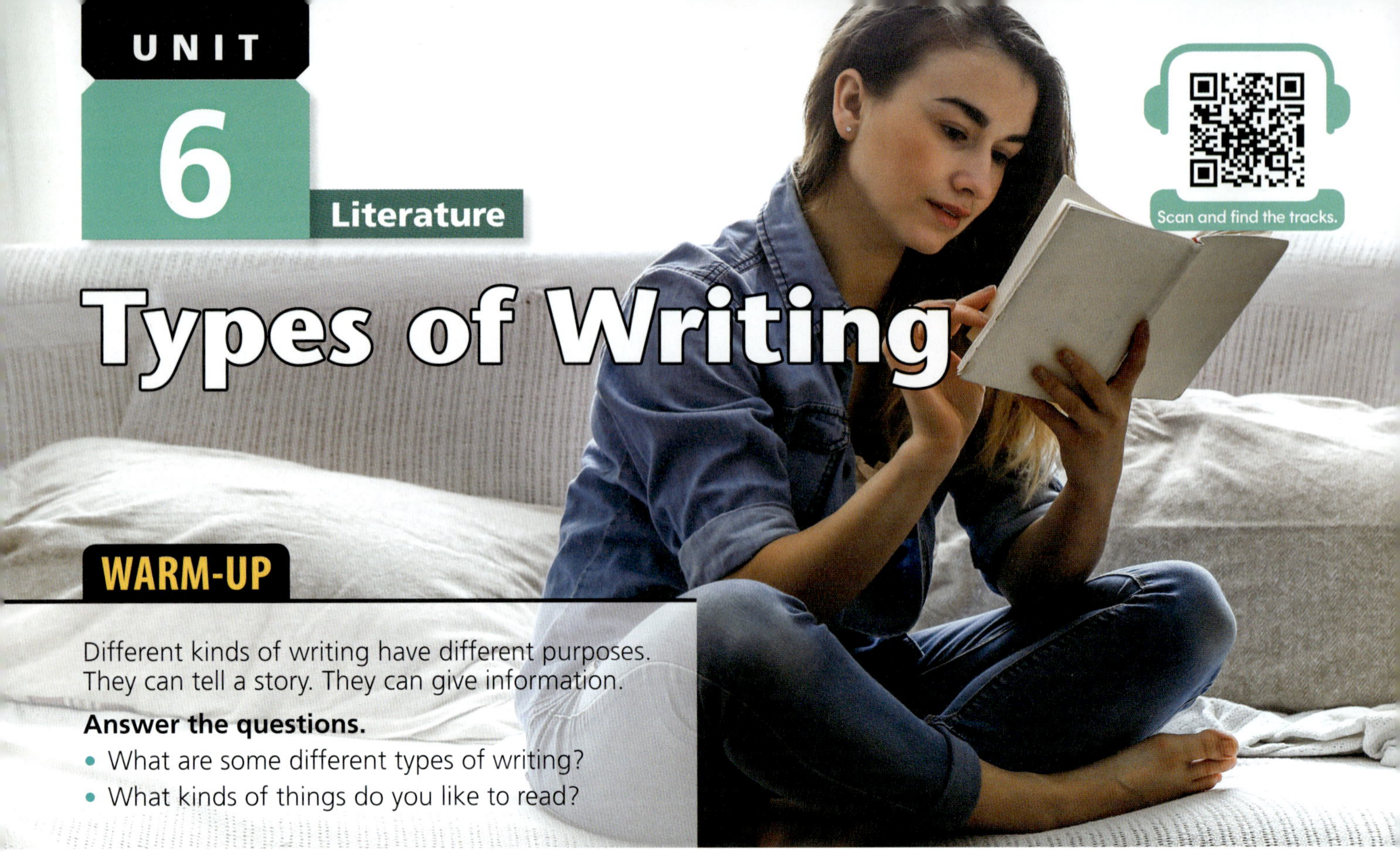

UNIT

6

Literature

Types of Writing

Scan and find the tracks.

WARM-UP

Different kinds of writing have different purposes. They can tell a story. They can give information.

Answer the questions.

- What are some different types of writing?
- What kinds of things do you like to read?

NEW WORDS

Track 12

Listen and match the word with its meaning.

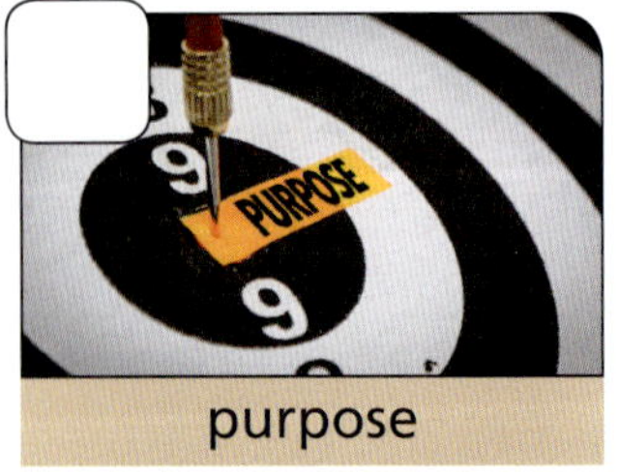

purpose

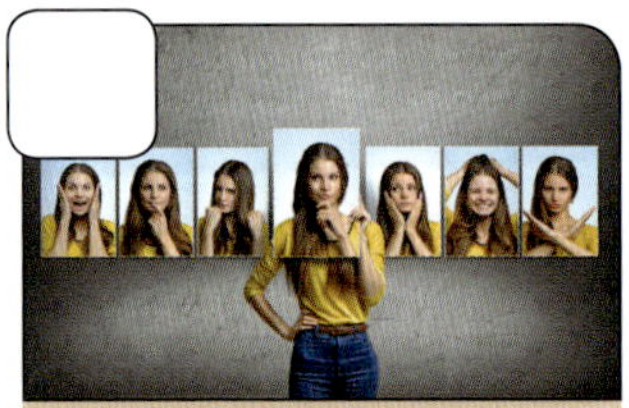
emotion

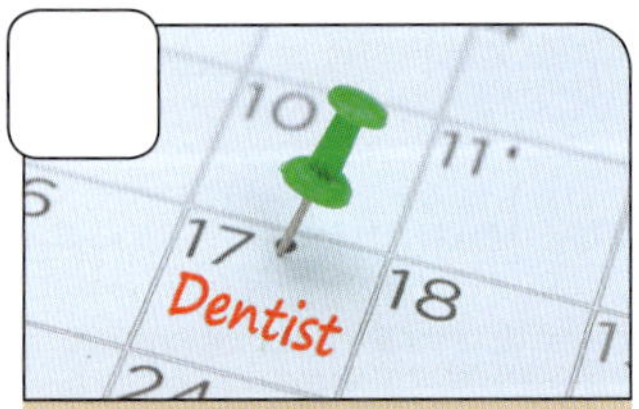

event

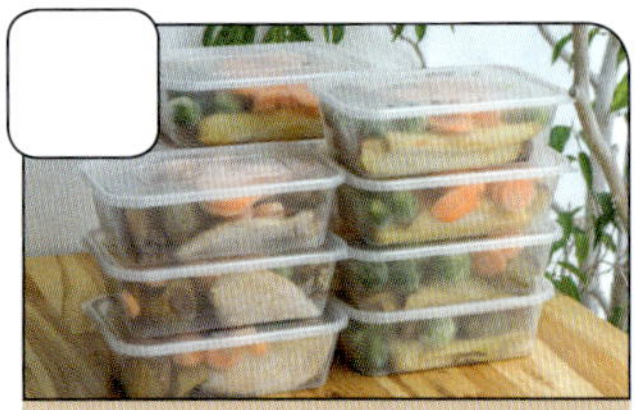
contain

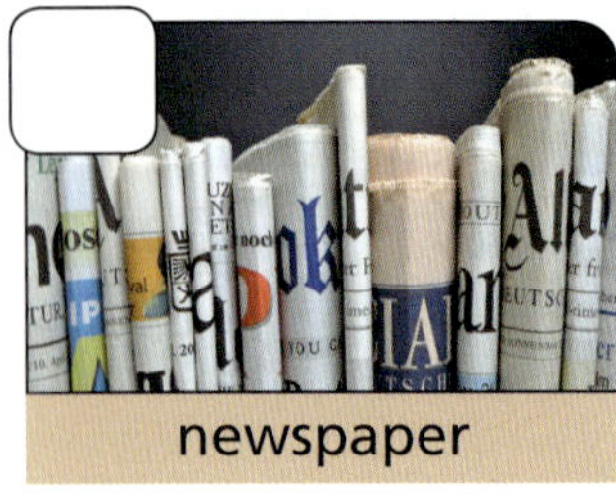

newspaper

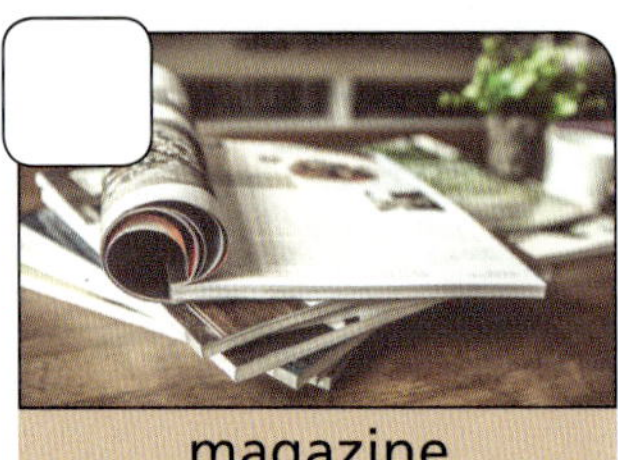

magazine

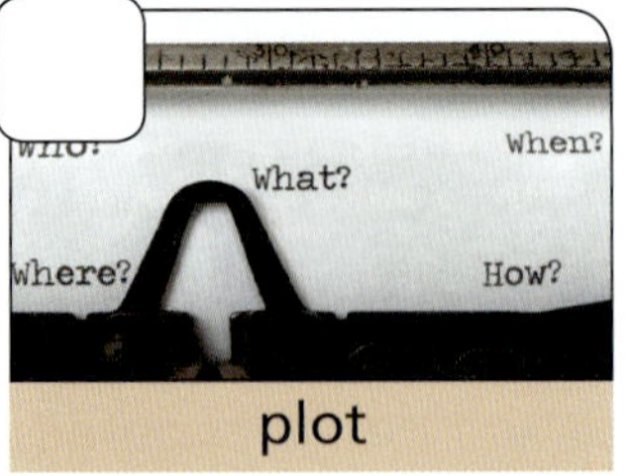

plot

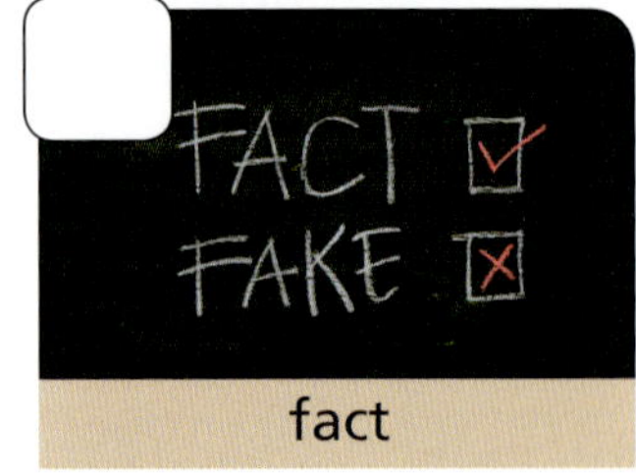

fact

1. a true piece of information
2. a weekly or monthly publication which has articles and photos
3. something important that happens
4. a feeling a person can have
5. to be made up of
6. the reason why something is done
7. a series of parts that come together to make the story in a novel, movie, etc.
8. a daily or weekly journal of current events

Listen and read.

Types of Writing

There are many ways to write, called formats. Different formats are used for different **purposes** of writing. They look different and make the readers think and feel different things.

Poetry is one format. It mixes language and **emotions**. Poems are created when words are formed into lines. Then a group of lines becomes a stanza. Lines sometimes rhyme at the end. This means that they have the same sound. For example:

It's a beautiful summer day.
All of the children can play.

The "-ay" sound rhymes at the end of both of these lines.

A novel is a book that usually **contains** characters. Novels have a **plot** and a sequence of **events**, and these come together to make the storyline. The setting is the place where the story happens.

An article is another format. It gives information and is often found in a **newspaper** or a **magazine**. It contains **facts** about a topic.

Take the time to read different formats of literature. You can enjoy different things with different formats.

Reading Time: _____ m _____ s / 170 words

VOCABULARY SKILLS

Two words can be joined together to make one **compound word**.

news+paper → **newspaper**

- **armchair**: a chair that has arms
- **eyeball**: the round part of the eye
- **firefighter**: a person who fights fires
- **pancake**: a flat cake cooked in a pan

READING SKILLS

Classifying

Classifying means putting things into groups that are related or have the same thing in common.

- The reading talks about three types of literature. Underline them.

READING COMPREHENSION

Choose the right answer.

1. What is the reading mainly about?
   a. Reading a novel
   b. Different kinds of writing
   c. The purpose of reading literature
   d. Ways to understand writing

2. Where can an article usually be found?
   a. In a novel
   b. In a poem
   c. In a format
   d. In a magazine

3. Which is NOT true according to the reading?
   a. An article is usually written with rhymes.
   b. A stanza is a group of lines.
   c. Poems use words and emotions.
   d. Novels usually contain characters.

READING SKILLS Classifying

Complete the chart with the correct information.

Poetry	Novels	Articles
1. _______________	3. _______________	5. _______________
_______________	_______________	_______________
2. _______________	4. _______________	6. _______________
_______________	_______________	_______________

a. Written in lines and stanzas   b. Found in newspapers
c. Have characters and a plot   d. Give information
e. Have a setting   f. Filled with emotions

VOCABULARY

Choose the right word to complete each sentence. There are two extra words.

| purpose   plot   emotions   magazine   contains   event   facts   newspaper |

1. My mother reads the _________________ each morning to learn what happened yesterday.

2. The _________________ of exercise is to stay healthy.

3. A wedding is an important _________________ for many people.

4. This novel _________________ 100 pages.

5. My favorite subject in school is science because I love learning interesting _________________ about our world.

6. We can tell someone's _________________ by the look on their face.

21st CENTURY SKILLS — Critical Thinking — Creativity — Collaboration — Communication

PROJECT Favorite Literature Types

You learned about different types of literature. Let's find out which type is the most popular in the class.

Step 1 On a sheet of paper, list the types of literature we have learned about. Put a number beside each of them to tell which one you like best (1, 2, 3). Your favorite type of literature will get a "1."

Sample Poetry = 3; Novels = 1; Articles = 2

____

Step 2 Think about why you like that type of literature best. Write a few sentences to explain.

Sample I like _novels_ best because _I like to read stories. I like to imagine myself in the story. I also like to guess what is going to happen next_.

I like _________________ best because ____

____.

Step 3 As a class, draw a chart on the board and put a mark under each student's favorite type of literature. Circle the most popular type in the class.

The Power of Poetry

WARM-UP

Poets spend a lot of their time trying to write a poem that will make readers think deeply. They choose every word carefully to do this.

Answer the questions.
- What do poets want readers to do?
- Why do poets choose their words carefully?

NEW WORDS Track 14

Listen and match the word with its meaning.

proverb

consider

appreciate

reflect

surface

early

soil

late

1. before the usual or expected time
2. part of the ground outside where plants can grow
3. the top part of something
4. after the usual or expected time
5. to think about deeply
6. a short, popular saying that gives advice
7. to value something
8. to think about something carefully before deciding

Listen and read.

The Power of Poetry

Poems help people think and feel different things. By reading poems, people can think and feel differently than normal. This is good because it helps people understand themselves and others better. A good example of this is a poem by Shel Silverstein called "Early Bird." It's about a well-known proverb: "The early bird catches the worm." This proverb tells us that it is good to be early for things because we'll get good things before others who are late.

By the end of "Early Bird," the poem makes us consider what happens to the worm in the proverb. The poet makes us reflect on this with his writing. Worms live underground. A worm that is living under the ground and comes up to the surface early in the morning is in danger. It will probably get picked up by a bird for breakfast. But another worm sleeps late and remains under the soil. It continues living safely and happily.

The poem is a good example of how to appreciate poetry.

> Reading Time: _____m _____s / 170 words

VOCABULARY SKILLS

Some common adverbs say when something happens. Many of them do not end in *-ly*.

- early → That bird wakes up **early**.
- late → Another worm sleeps **late**.
- then → I'll see you **then**!
- today → We don't have math class **today**.

READING SKILLS

Cause & Effect

Identifying cause and effect helps us understand why something happens (the cause) and what happens (the effect).

- Circle the causes and <u>underline</u> the effects found in the reading.

READING COMPREHENSION

Choose the right answer.

1. What is the reading mainly about?
   a. The poet Shel Silverstein
   b. A poem that makes you reflect on life
   c. Ways birds can trick worms
   d. Reasons it is best for us to sleep late

2. A worm that ___________ is more likely to get eaten.
   a. looks for food
   b. sleeps late
   c. wakes up early
   d. stays under the soil

3. What is NOT true according to the reading?
   a. Sleeping late is best for a bird to get food.
   b. Birds eat worms that are on the top of the soil.
   c. Many people think it's good to be early.
   d. Worms that stay under the soil are safer.

READING SKILLS **Cause & Effect**

Complete the chart with the correct information.

	Cause	
	Sleeping Late	**Waking Up Early**
Bird	1. _______________	2. _______________
Worm	3. _______________	4. _______________

Effect

a. Gets eaten
b. Does not get eaten
c. Gets a worm for breakfast
d. Does not get a worm for breakfast

VOCABULARY

Choose the right word to complete each sentence. There are two extra words.

early	late	consider	soil	proverb	surface	reflect	appreciate

1. We ate a(n) _________________ lunch at 11 o'clock.

2. I was _________________ for school this morning because I missed the bus.

3. "Better late than never" is a well-known _________________ which reminds us to do important things, even if we're late.

4. A leaf floated on the _________________ of the water.

5. The audio guide in the museum helps you _________________ each work better.

6. Let's dig up some _________________ and plant this tree.

21st CENTURY SKILLS — Critical Thinking · Creativity · Collaboration · Communication

PROJECT Read More Poems

You read about the poem "Early Bird." Let's look at another poem by Shel Silverstein and see how we feel about it.

Step 1 Find and read a poem by Shel Silverstein.

Shel Silverstein poems 🔍

The Land of Happy

Pancake?

Snowball

Step 2 Write what you think about the poem.

Sample I read "_The Land of Happy_." _I love this poem because it is honest. Sometimes it looks like everyone in the world is happy. But this is not always true_.

I read "_________________." _________________

____

Step 3 Present your thoughts to the class.

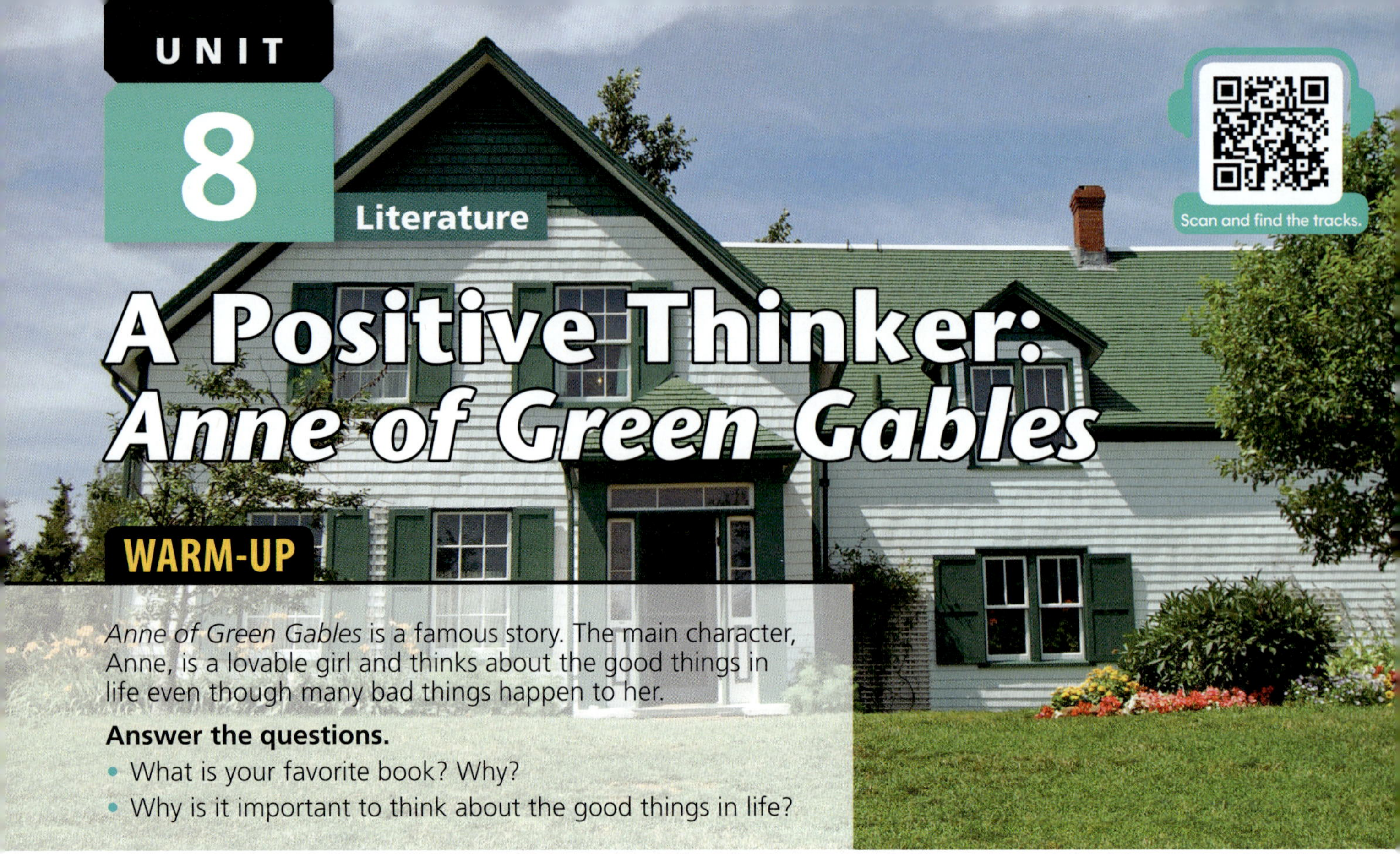

UNIT 8

Literature

A Positive Thinker: *Anne of Green Gables*

Scan and find the tracks.

WARM-UP

Anne of Green Gables is a famous story. The main character, Anne, is a lovable girl and thinks about the good things in life even though many bad things happen to her.

Answer the questions.

- What is your favorite book? Why?
- Why is it important to think about the good things in life?

NEW WORDS

Track 16

Listen and match the word with its meaning.

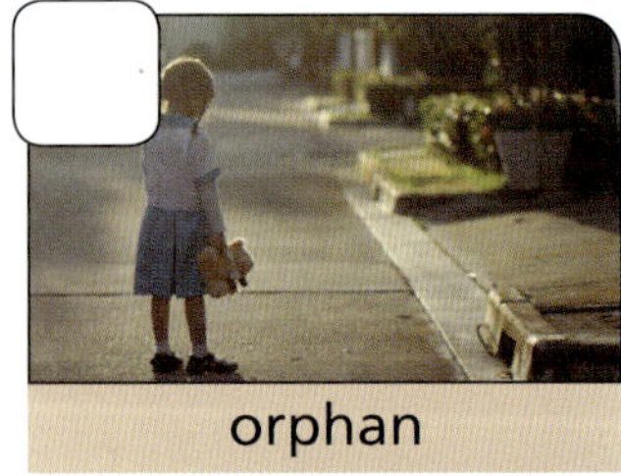

orphan

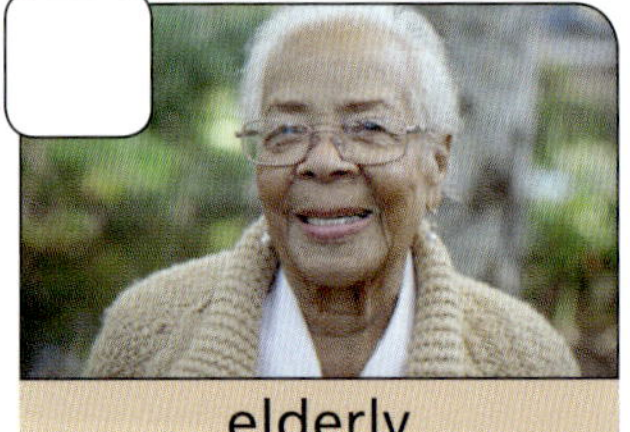

elderly

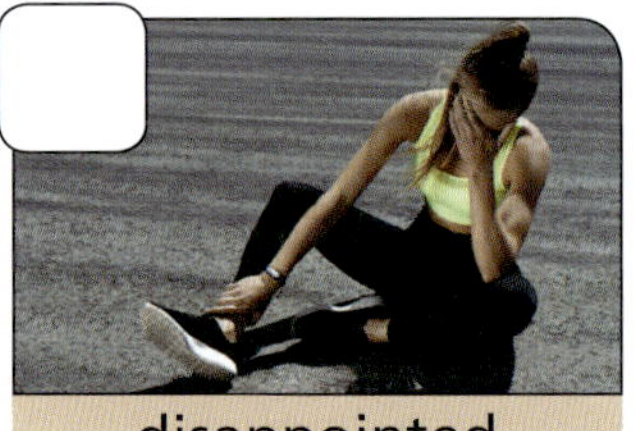

disappointed

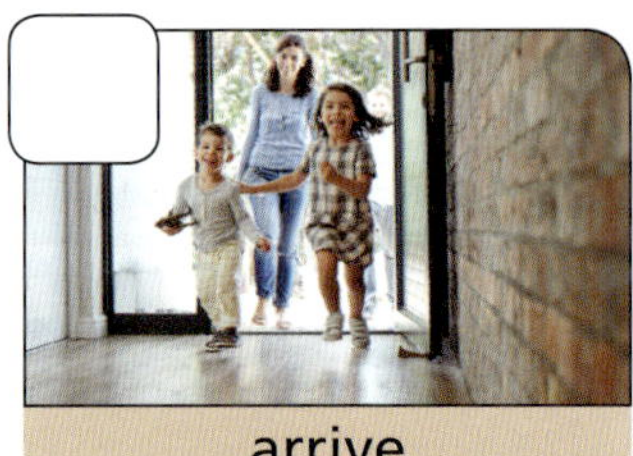

arrive

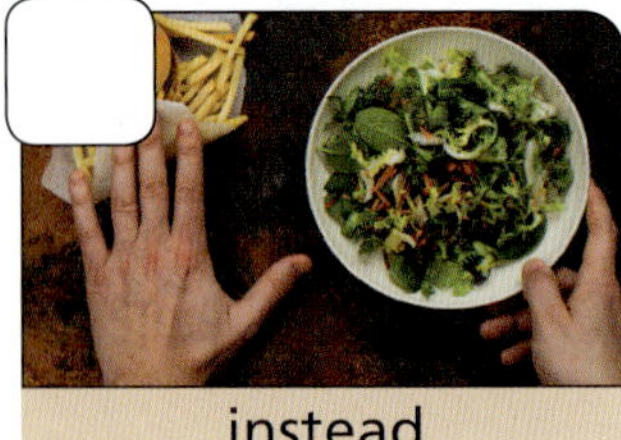

instead

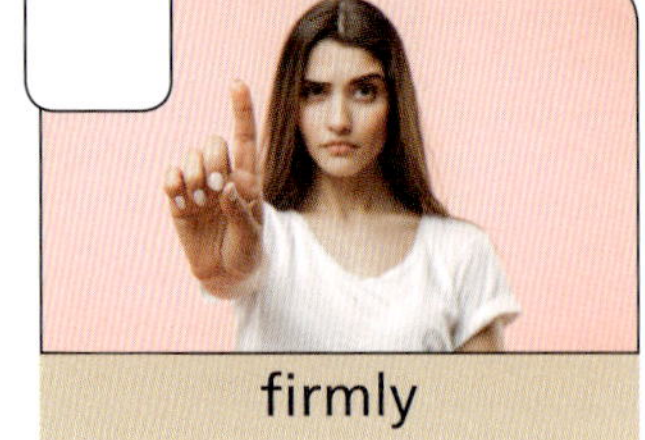

firmly

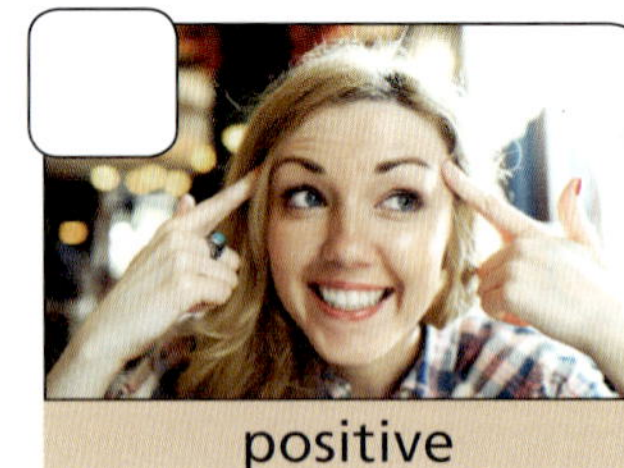

positive

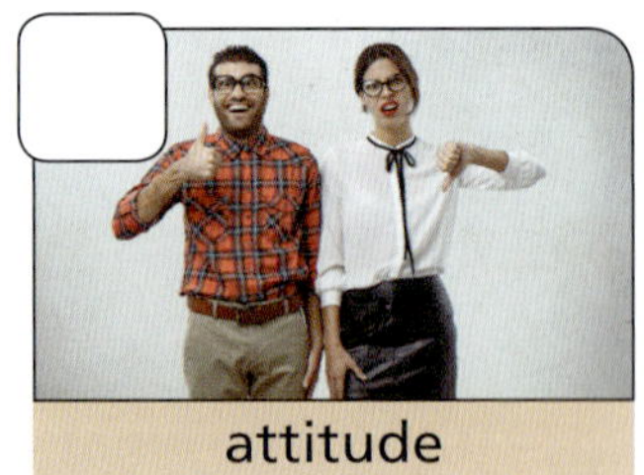

attitude

1. a polite way to say "old"
2. to reach a place you are going to
3. used to say that one thing is done or chosen over another choice
4. a way you think or feel that you show in your actions
5. a child who has no parents
6. thinking of the good side of things
7. strongly; not in a weak or uncertain way
8. sad or unhappy because something was not as good as you hoped

A Positive Thinker: *Anne of Green Gables*

Anne of *Green Gables* was written by L. M. Montgomery in Canada. It was first published in 1908. It is a story about an **orphan** girl who helps change the lives of people around her.

The story begins with an **elderly** man, Matthew, and woman, Marilla. They live together on their farm, which is called Green Gables. They want to adopt a boy to help them on the farm. They are **disappointed** when a girl **arrives instead**. At first, they want to send Anne back to the orphanage. However, Anne is interesting, so Matthew and Marilla decide to wait.

Anne has a **positive attitude**. She can find good in any situation. Anne says, "You can always enjoy things if you make up your mind **firmly** that you will." After spending just one day with Anne, Matthew and Marilla decide to have Anne stay at Green Gables. That decision changes all three of their lives for the better. They are filled with love, happiness, and appreciation.

Reading Time: _____m _____s / 164 words

VOCABULARY SKILLS

The suffix **-sion** is used to turn verbs into nouns.

decide+sion → deci**sion**

- discus**sion**: the act of talking about something
- conclu**sion**: the end of an event or process
- expres**sion**: the act of making your thoughts or feelings known

READING SKILLS

Main Idea & Details

Some stories and reading passages are organized according to a main idea and the details that give more information about the main idea.

- Circle the main idea of the reading.
- <u>Underline</u> three details about the main character.

READING COMPREHENSION

Choose the right answer.

1. What is the reading mainly about?
- a. The writer of *Anne of Green Gables*
- b. How to have a positive attitude in every situation
- c. How *Anne of Green Gables* is liked around the world
- d. The story of a girl who is adopted by an old man and woman

2. Why were Matthew and Marilla disappointed when Anne arrived?
- a. She had a bad attitude.
- b. They had wanted to adopt a boy.
- c. She had no parents.
- d. They thought she was too young.

3. Which is NOT true according to the reading?
- a. Anne was an unhappy girl.
- b. Matthew and Marilla were old.
- c. Anne came from an orphanage.
- d. Matthew and Marilla finally adopted Anne.

READING SKILLS Main Idea & Details

Complete the chart with the correct information.

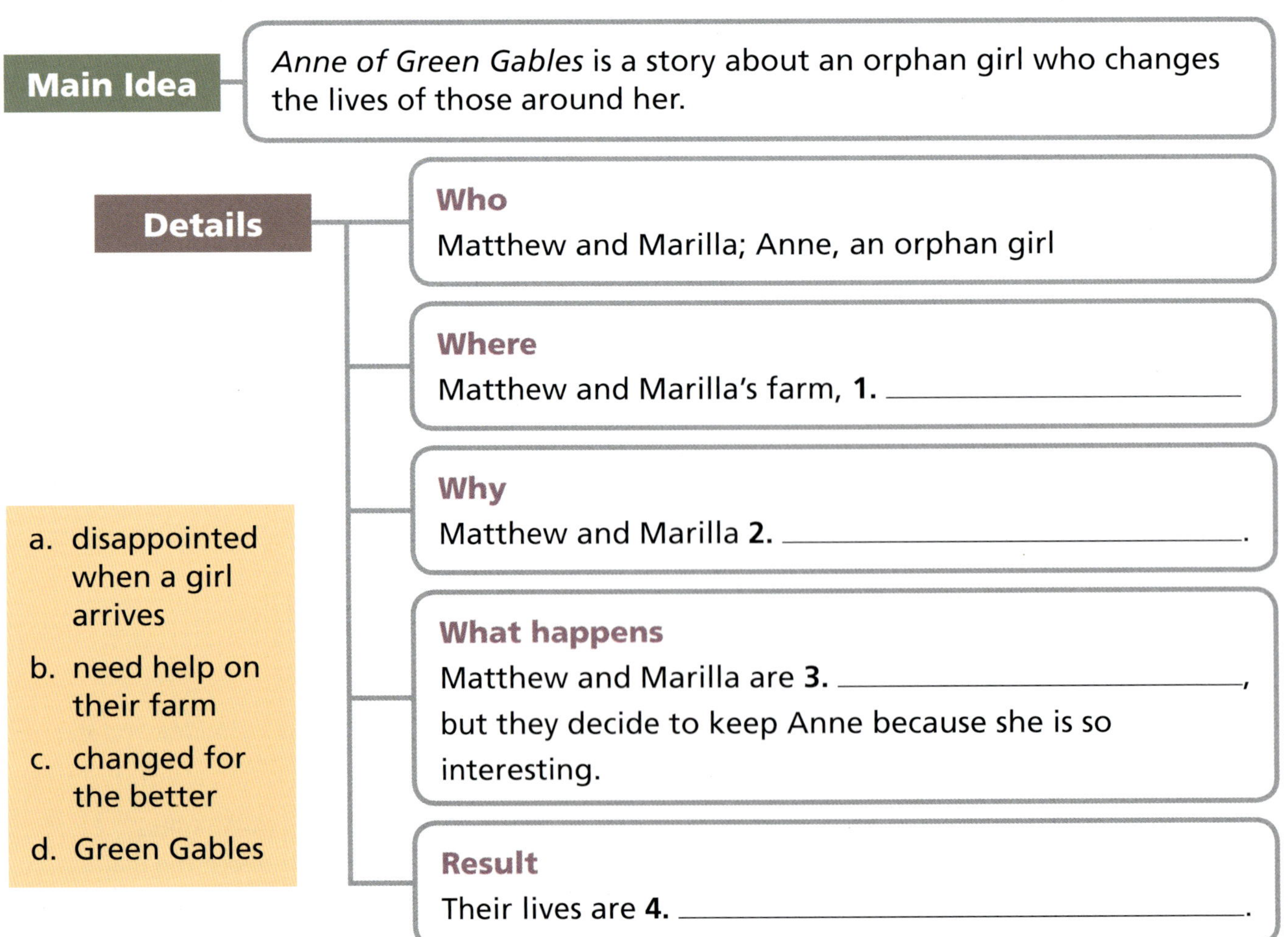

VOCABULARY

Choose the right word to complete each sentence. There are two extra words.

| orphan | elderly | disappointed | arrives | firmly | instead | positive | attitude |

1. Shawn has a bad ___________________ about singing in the school play. He doesn't even try.

2. Pam was ___________________ when she lost the race.

3. The nice man helped the slow, ___________________ woman cross the street.

4. Nick is very ___________________, so he is always smiling.

5. We were going to have chicken for dinner, but we decided to have pizza ___________________.

6. When Grandma ___________________ at our house, we are going out to eat dinner.

21st CENTURY SKILLS · Critical Thinking · Creativity · Collaboration · Communication

PROJECT An Interesting Character

Anne is the main character in *Anne of Green Gables*. She is a funny girl with interesting qualities. Now, let's talk about a character in your favorite book.

Step 1 Think about your favorite book. Describe an interesting character from that book.

Sample My favorite book is _Matilda_. The character that I am going to talk about is _Miss Trunchbull_. She is _the headmistress of Matilda's school_ and _she is always very angry and mean_. She is interesting because _she does not like children but still she runs a school_.

My favorite book is ___________________. The character that I am going to talk about is ___________________

___________________. (He / She) is ___________________

and ___________________. (He / She) is interesting because ___________________

___________________.

Step 2 Draw a picture of the character.

Step 3 Tell your class about the character.

9 — Economics

Digital Money

WARM-UP

How do you usually pay for things you buy? Someday you may not have to carry any money at all. It may all be on your computer or tablet.

Answer the questions.
- Why do people carry around money?
- Do you think using computer money will be easier than carrying paper money and coins? Why or why not?

NEW WORDS 

Listen and match the word with its meaning.

cash

card

check

coin

method

recently

increasingly

security

1. money in the form of small, flat, and usually round pieces of metal
2. not long ago
3. money in the form of bills and coins
4. a way of doing something
5. more and more
6. a piece of paper that is used to make a payment to someone using the money in a bank account
7. safety
8. a special piece of plastic used for paying for things

Listen and read.

Digital Money

People usually carry around cash, checks, coins, and cards to pay for things. They have used these methods to pay for things for a very long time. But recently, people carry less cash, checks, and coins than before.

Increasingly, people are using only cards and online banking. By using only cards, people carry less paper money and coins. But they still need to bring their cards with them.

Another type of digital money is through online payment companies. Of course, banks have websites and apps. But there are online payment companies, like PayPal, that are used to pay for things. People can get, save, and spend money without ever seeing or touching it. They also don't have to carry around anything but their smartphone.

Very recently, an even newer form of digital money has emerged. It is called crypto-currency. The number of people and businesses who accept digital money is increasing. But people are worried about security. They want to be sure that their digital money is safe.

Reading Time: ______ m ______ s / 168 words

VOCABULARY SKILLS

Some adverbs are used before a comparative form to mean "very." "Very" cannot be used before a comparative.

An **even** newer form of digital money has emerged.

- far: Those shoes are **far** more expensive.
- much: Flying is **much** safer than driving.
- a lot: Digital currency will become **a lot** more popular.

READING SKILLS

Main Idea & Details

The main idea is the topic of a piece of writing. It is what the writing is mostly about. The main idea is often found in the first few sentences. The other sentences are the details. They give more information about the main idea.

- Circle the main idea in the reading.
- Underline two main details that support the main idea.

READING COMPREHENSION

Choose the right answer.

1. What is the reading mainly about?
   a. Digital money
   b. Cash and checks
   c. Cards and banks
   d. Worries about security

2. These days, most people __________.
   a. carry a lot of cash
   b. rarely use credit cards
   c. don't use checks very much
   d. like cash more than digital money

3. Which is NOT true according to the reading?
   a. It is easy to get digital money for free.
   b. Digital money is becoming more popular.
   c. People want to make sure digital money is secure.
   d. The number of businesses that take digital money will increase.

READING SKILLS Main Idea & Details

Complete the chart with the correct information.

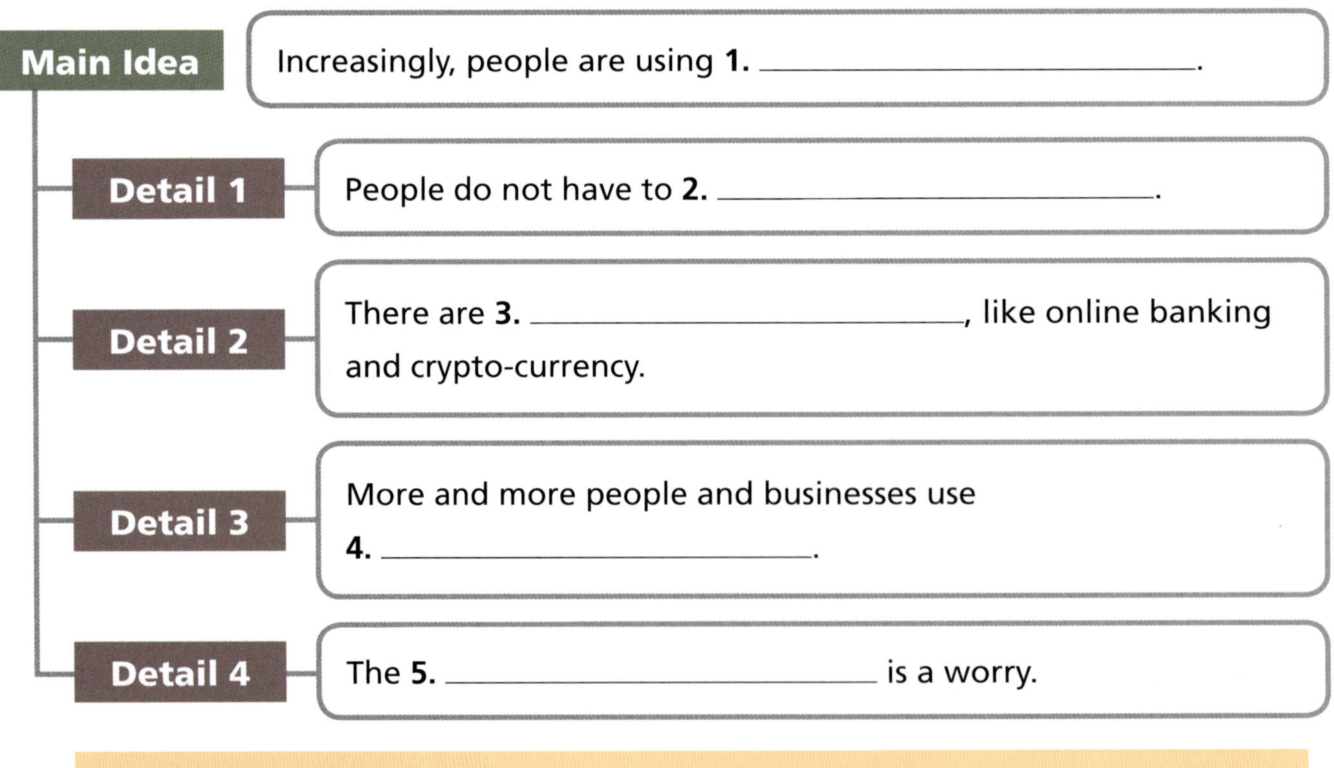

VOCABULARY

Choose the right word to complete each sentence. There are two extra words.

| increasingly | cash | coins | method | card | check | recently | security |

1. To buy things online, you need a(n) _________________. You cannot pay with cash.
2. This book isn't old. It was _________________ published.
3. The soda machine takes bills and _________________.
4. Because of new technology, we can do things _________________ faster.
5. The _________________ check at the airport took a long time. They want to keep passengers safe.
6. You can pay by _________________ or card.

21st CENTURY SKILLS

Critical Thinking · Creativity · Collaboration · Communication

PROJECT Create Digital Money

You read about the use of digital money. Now, let's create a digital payment system.

Step 1 Work in small groups. Create a digital payment system to be used by students in our school. Give it a name.

Sample Our digital payment system is called _SchoolPal_.

Our digital payment system is called _________________.

Step 2 Make a plan that tells how the system works.

Sample Students go to _the SchoolPal website_. They can get _$20 in their smartphones each week_. They can use the money _to buy lunch, snacks, and school things in our school only_. _SchoolPal_ will take the payment _from the amount in their smartphones_.

Students go to _________________. They can get _________________. They can use the money _________________. _________________ will take the payment _________________.

Step 3 Present your plan to the class and discuss how it works.

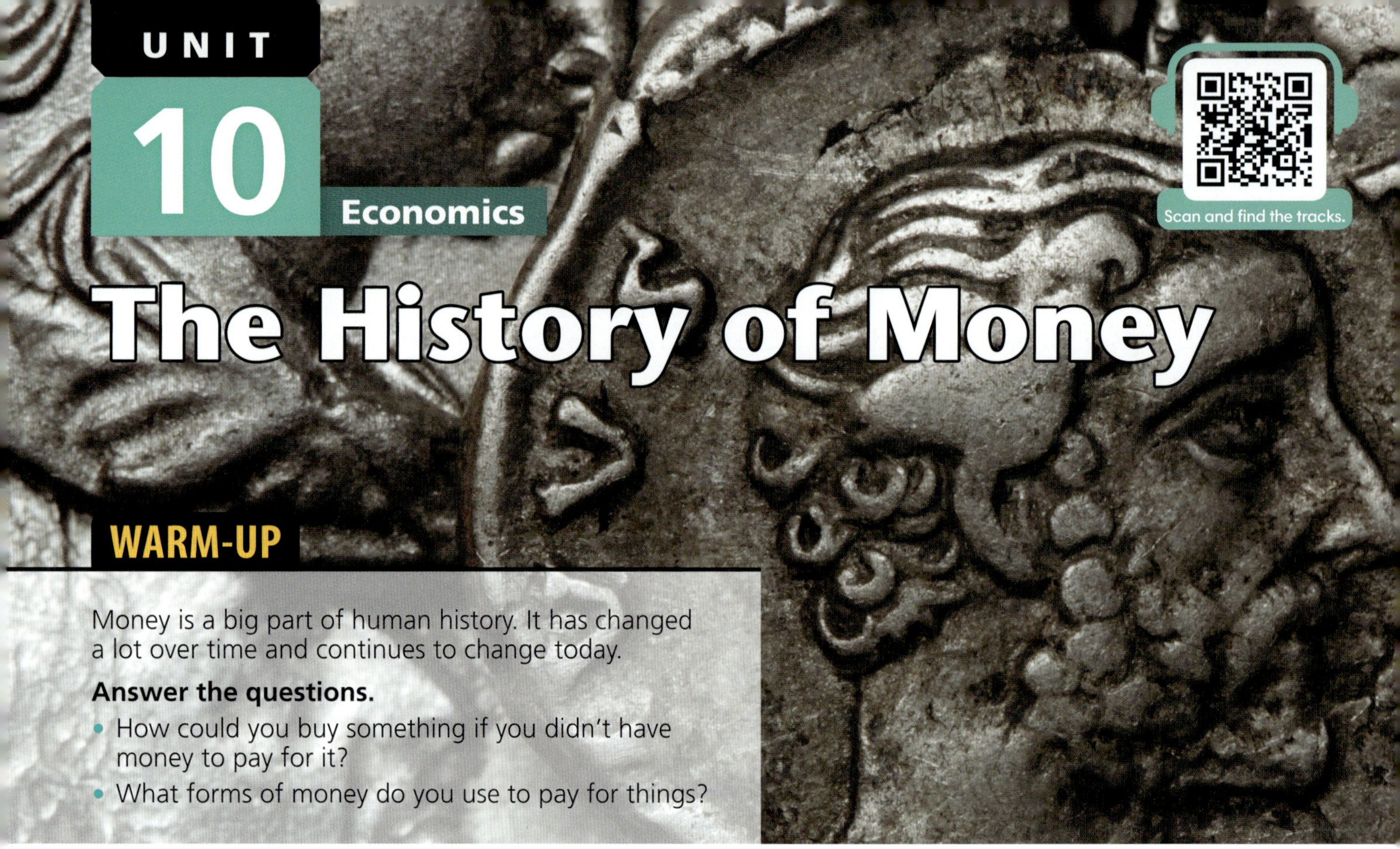

UNIT 10

Economics

Scan and find the tracks.

The History of Money

WARM-UP

Money is a big part of human history. It has changed a lot over time and continues to change today.

Answer the questions.

- How could you buy something if you didn't have money to pay for it?
- What forms of money do you use to pay for things?

NEW WORDS

Track 20

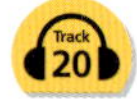

Listen and match the word with its meaning.

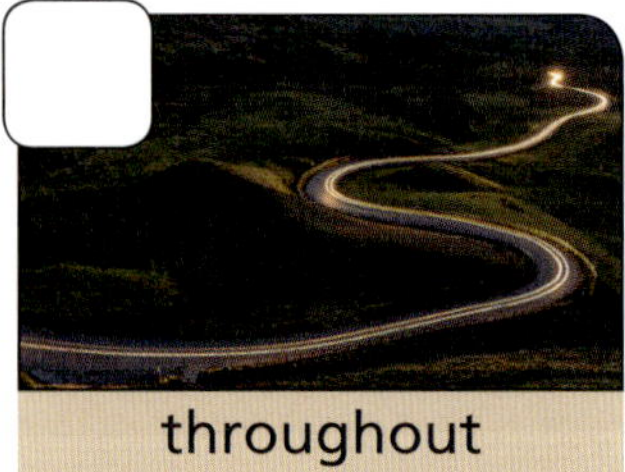

throughout

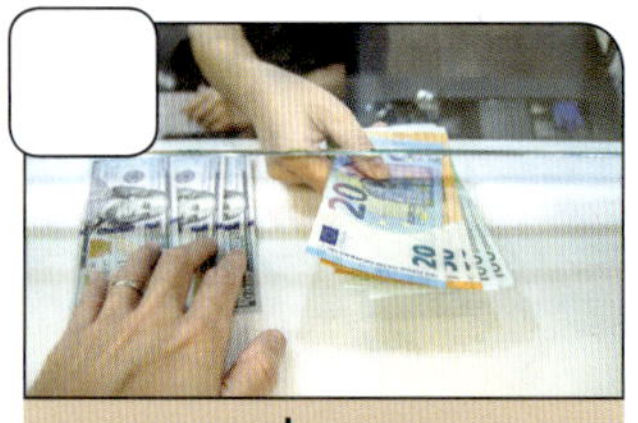

exchange

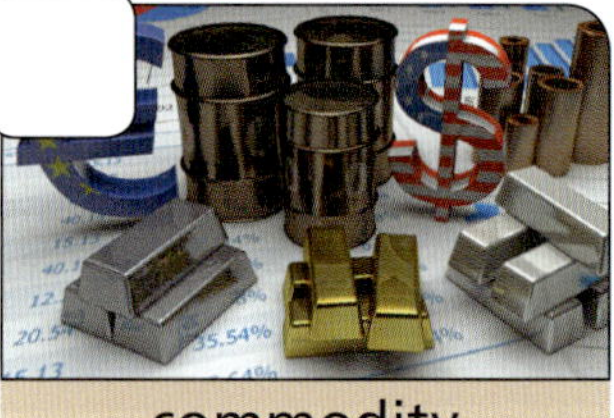

commodity

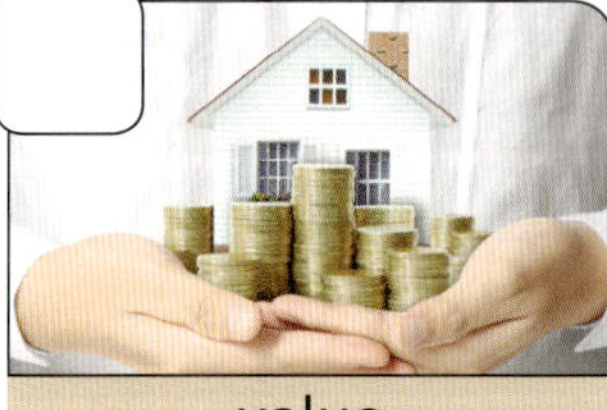

value

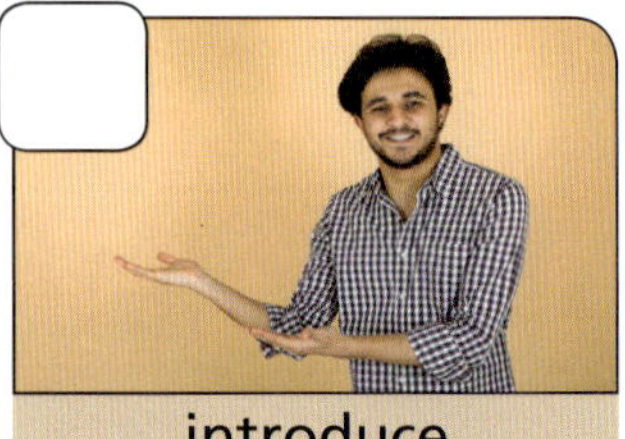

introduce

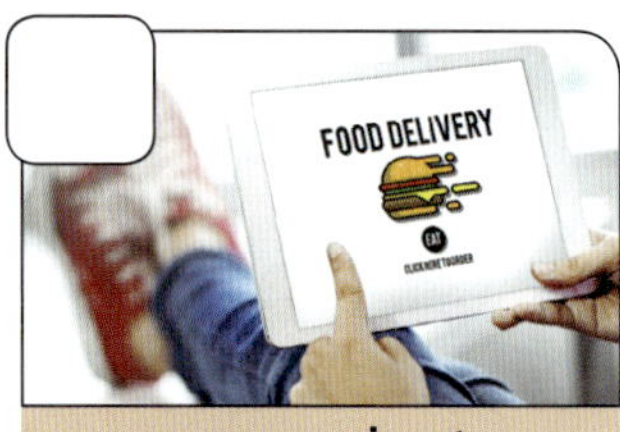

convenient

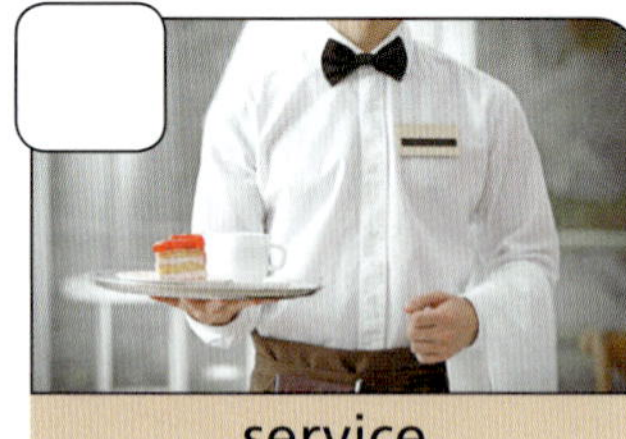

service

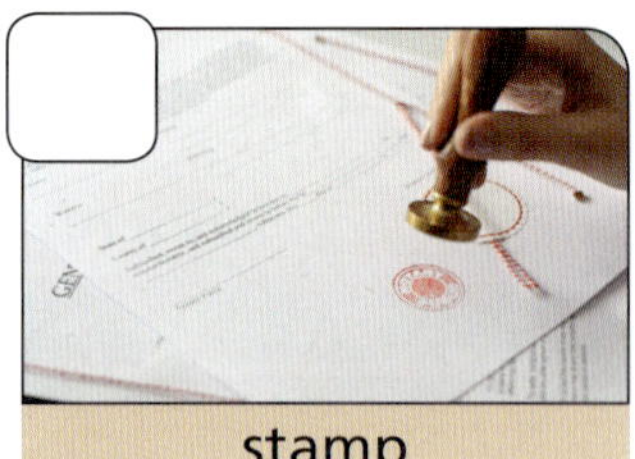

stamp

1. allowing you to do something easily or without trouble
2. something you can sell for money
3. to mark by pressing a design onto the surface
4. during every part of
5. how important, useful, or expensive something is
6. to give something and get something back
7. work done by an individual or group
8. to bring a plan, system, or product into use for the first time

The History of Money

How we pay for things has changed a lot **throughout** history. Humans have tried to make paying for things easier and easier. This continues on today.

A long time ago, people **exchanged** goods and **services** to pay for things. They exchanged something valuable they had for something else they needed or wanted. However, this only worked if both people wanted what the other person had. So, eventually, **commodities** became money. Commodities are things that most people need, such as cows, plants, salt, and cloth.

Then, about 3,300 years ago, metal coins were **introduced** as money. The **value** of each coin was **stamped** on it. Coins made paying for things easier. Everyone easily understood the value of coins. Also, coins tend to last a lot longer than many commodities.

Around 800 CE, paper money was made. Paper is lighter than coins and is very easy to transport. Today, people still use paper money and coins. They also use cards and digital money now. Money continues to become more **convenient**.

> **Reading Time:** _____ m _____ s / 168 words

VOCABULARY SKILLS

Some verbs have irregular forms in the past tense.

- understand → understood
- have → had
- become → became
- make → made
- lose → lost

READING SKILLS

Sequencing

Sequencing is used to put a series of events in order. The information is usually arranged according to time. Some words that are used in this type of writing are *first, next, then, in the past, today, now, in the future*, etc. Dates can also be used.

- <u>Underline</u> the words in the reading that give clues about the sequence of the events.

READING COMPREHENSION

Choose the right answer.

1. What is the reading mainly about?
    a. Who developed the first forms of money
    b. Why people need paper and metal money
    c. The most common commodities around the world
    d. The different ways people have paid for things over time

2. Why is paper money easier to use than coins?
    a. It is not as heavy.
    b. It never changes.
    c. It is very valuable.
    d. It is used by many countries.

3. Which is NOT true according to the reading?
    a. People now can use digital money to buy things.
    b. Paper money was developed before metal coins.
    c. Paper money is still used today.
    d. People used to exchange goods before money was invented.

READING SKILLS Sequencing

Complete the chart with the correct information.

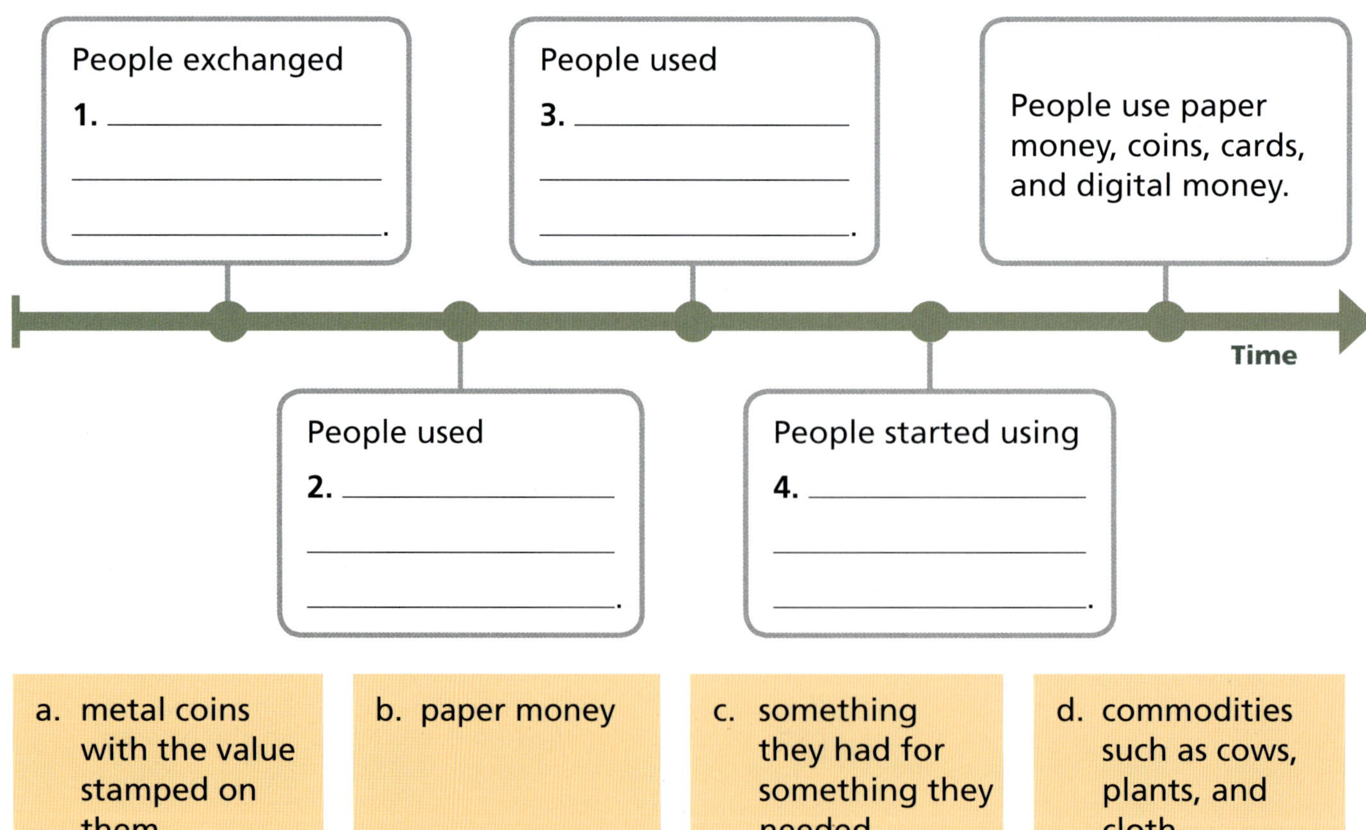

VOCABULARY

Choose the right word to complete each sentence. There are two extra words.

throughout   exchanged   commodity   services   introduced   convenient   value   stamped

1. Taking the bus is more _____________________ than walking.

2. The post office _____________________ the envelope with the date it was mailed.

3. Rice is a basic _____________________ all around the world.

4. The students _____________________ phone numbers, so they could call each other later.

5. I _____________________ my brother to a new kind of snack.

6. The little boy cried _____________________ his sister's dance performance.

21st CENTURY SKILLS   Critical Thinking   Creativity   Collaboration   Communication

PROJECT Design New Money

You learned how money has changed over the years. The design of money also changes, such as the images on paper money. Now, let's try to design some money.

Step 1 Look at some paper money from your country. Choose one bill and think about how you would change it.

What image would you put on the front of the bill? _____________________________________

Why? ____

What image would you put on the back of the bill? _____________________________________

Why? ____

Step 2 Draw the front and back sides of the bill.

Step 3 Show your bill to the class, and explain your design.

Sample   I chose to design a new _$100_ bill. On the front side of the bill, I would put an image of _an eagle_. That's because _the eagle is an important symbol of my country_. On the back side of the bill, I would put an image of _stars and stripes_. That's because _they represent freedom to me_.

I chose to design a new _____________________________ bill. On the front side of the bill, I would put an image of _____________________________. That's because _____________________________ _____________________________________. On the back side of the bill, I would put an image of _____________________________. That's because _____________________________________.

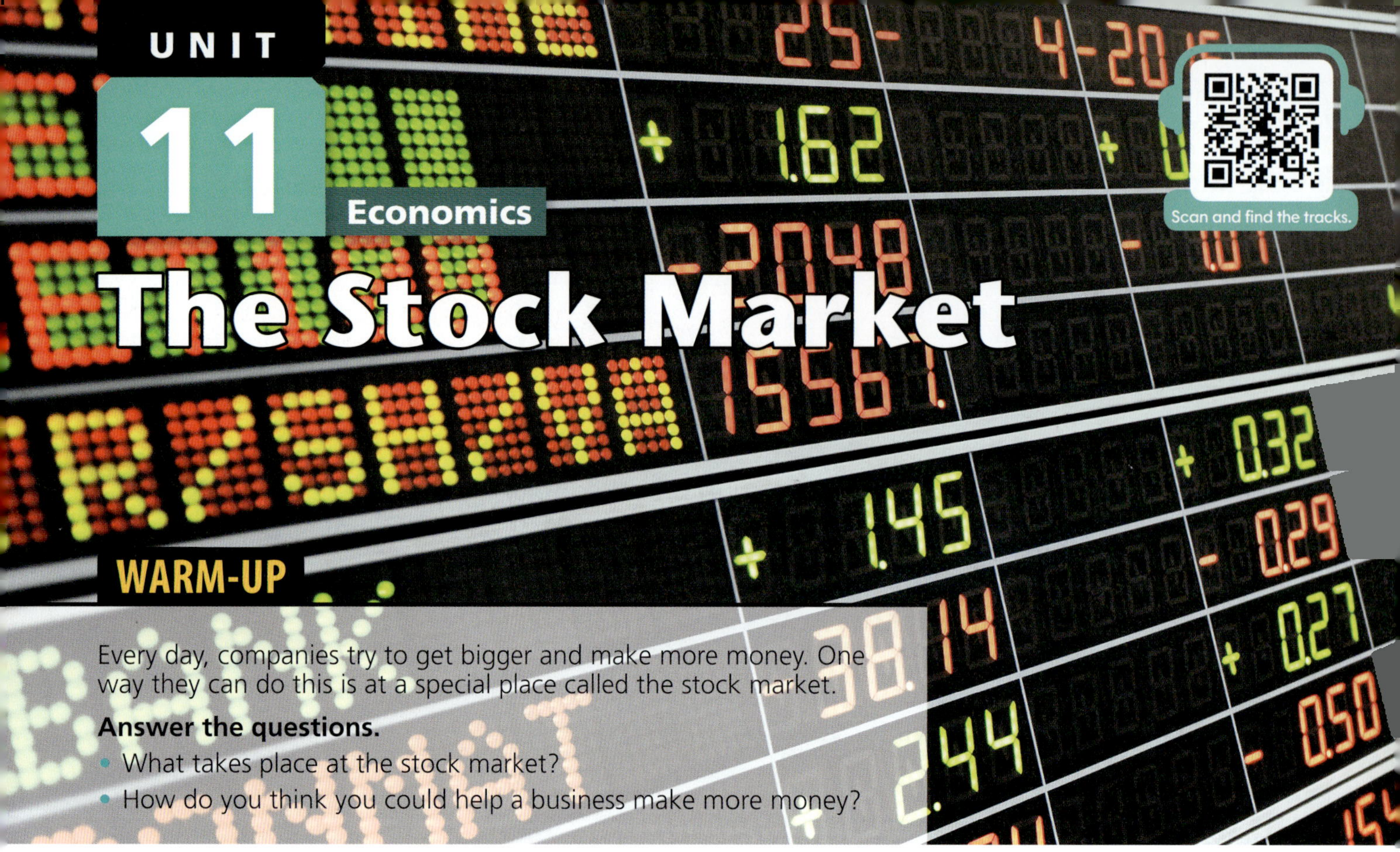

UNIT 11

Economics

The Stock Market

Scan and find the tracks.

WARM-UP

Every day, companies try to get bigger and make more money. One way they can do this is at a special place called the stock market.

Answer the questions.

- What takes place at the stock market?
- How do you think you could help a business make more money?

NEW WORDS

Track 22

Listen and match the word with its meaning.

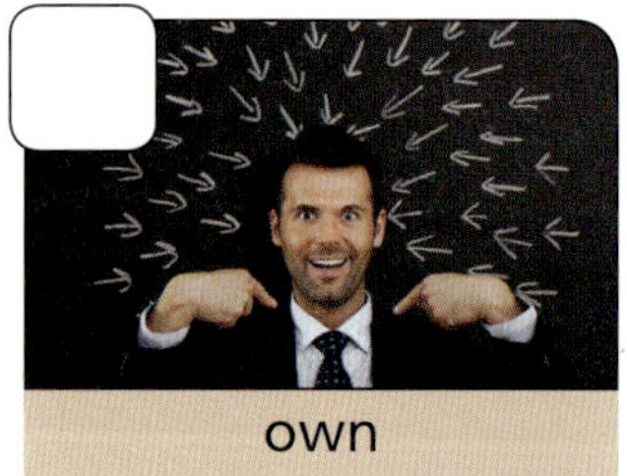

own

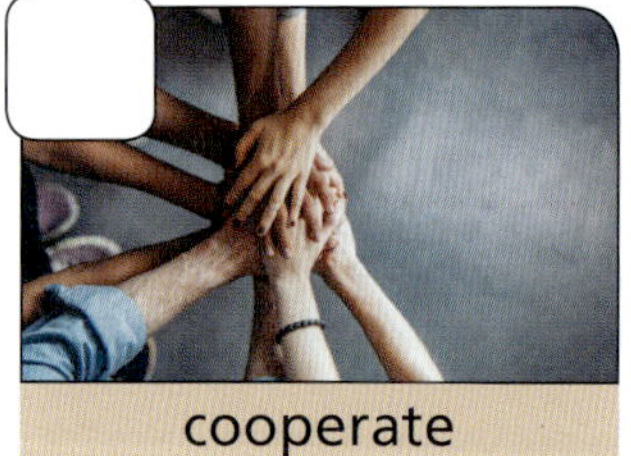

cooperate

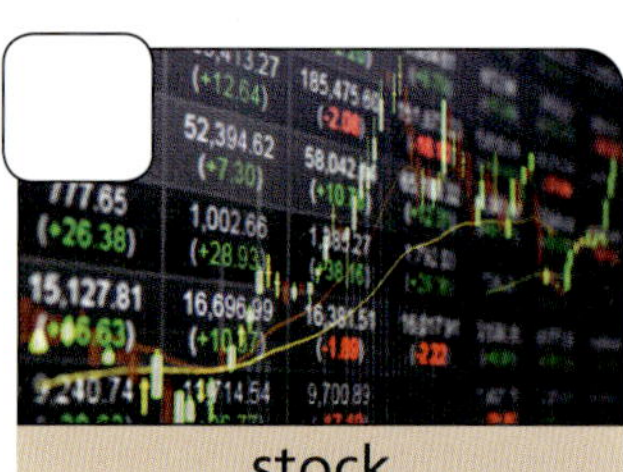

stock

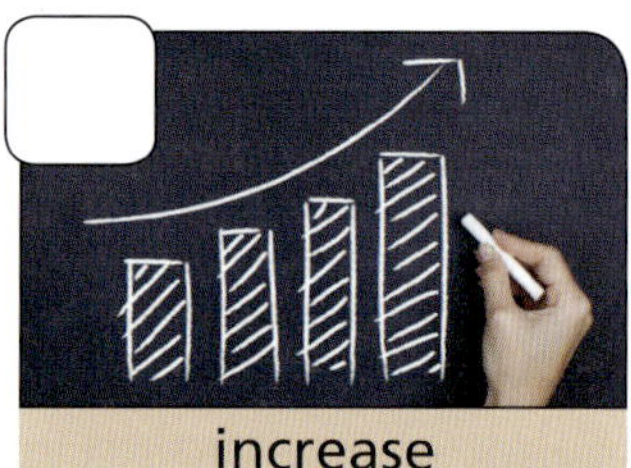

increase

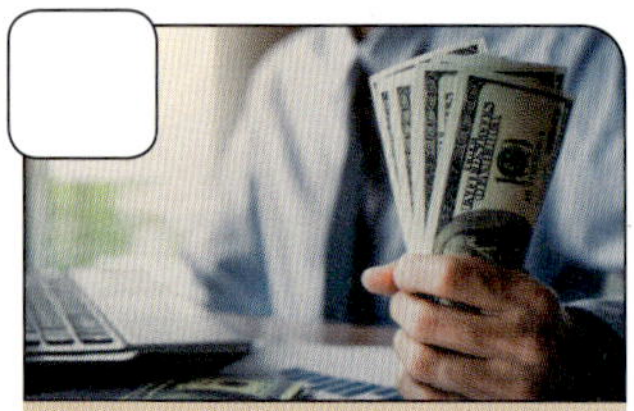

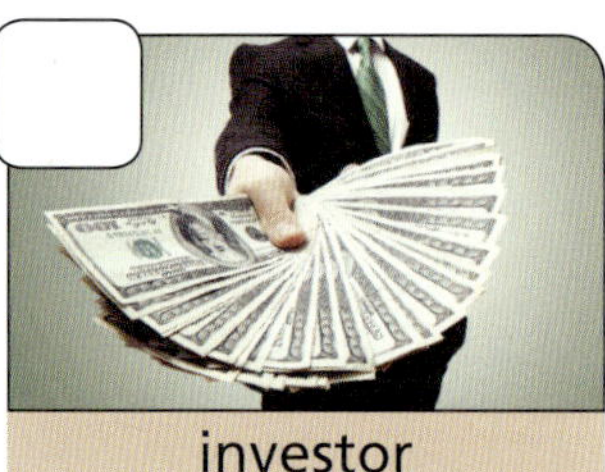

profit

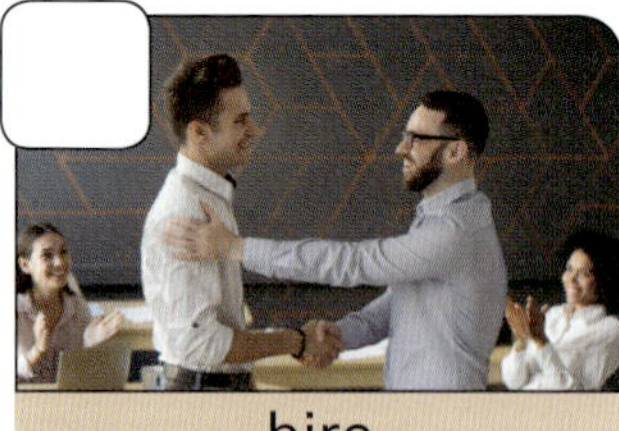

investor

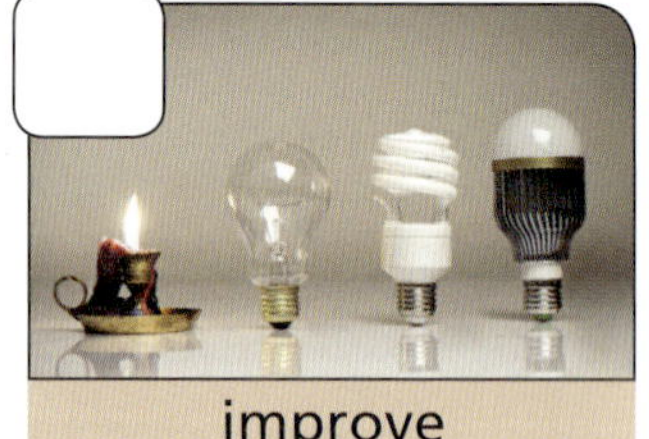

hire

improve

1. to work together
2. to make someone or something better
3. to grow in size, amount, number, etc.
4. to have something that belongs to you
5. one of the parts of a business that shows the value of the company
6. money that is made in a business
7. to give a job to someone and pay them for doing work
8. a person who uses their money to make more money

Listen and read.

The Stock Market

The **stock** market is a place where people buy and sell stocks. Stocks are small parts of a company that people can buy, **own**, and sell. Businesses and people go to the stock market to **cooperate** and try to make money together.

For many people, their goal is to buy a stock and wait for its value to **increase**. Then they sell it later for **profits**. These people are called **investors**. In a stock market, the values of stocks go up and down every day. Investors can sell their stocks at any time. They try to choose the best time to sell for profits.

The stock market is good for businesses, too. Companies who have many investors can do things like create newer and better goods and also **hire** more

workers. This helps them to make profits. They use money from investors to **improve** their company and make it more valuable. This is how companies and investors work together to try to make profits in the stock market.

> **Reading Time:** ______ m ______ s / 168 words

VOCABULARY SKILLS

The prefix **co-** at the beginning of a word means "together."

co+operate → **co**operate

- **co**write: to write something together
- **co**worker: someone whom you work with
- **co**-owner: one of two or more people who own something together

READING SKILLS

Sequencing

When we read, the information is organized in a special order. It helps us understand the sequence of events.

What would happen after the values of stocks that investors buy go up?

- <u>Underline</u> the sentence in the reading.

READING COMPREHENSION

Choose the right answer.

1. What is the reading mainly about?
- a. How businesses get profits
- b. What the stock market is
- c. How a large business works
- d. How investors hire workers

2. Why do investors put money into a company?
- a. To get more money back
- b. To give money to the company
- c. To buy goods
- d. To take money from the company

3. Which is NOT true according to the reading?
- a. Selling stocks is a way to get money to improve a business.
- b. The stocks of a business are sold at supermarkets.
- c. People who buy stocks are called investors.
- d. Buying stocks can be a good way to earn money.

READING SKILLS **Sequencing**

Complete the chart with the correct sentences.

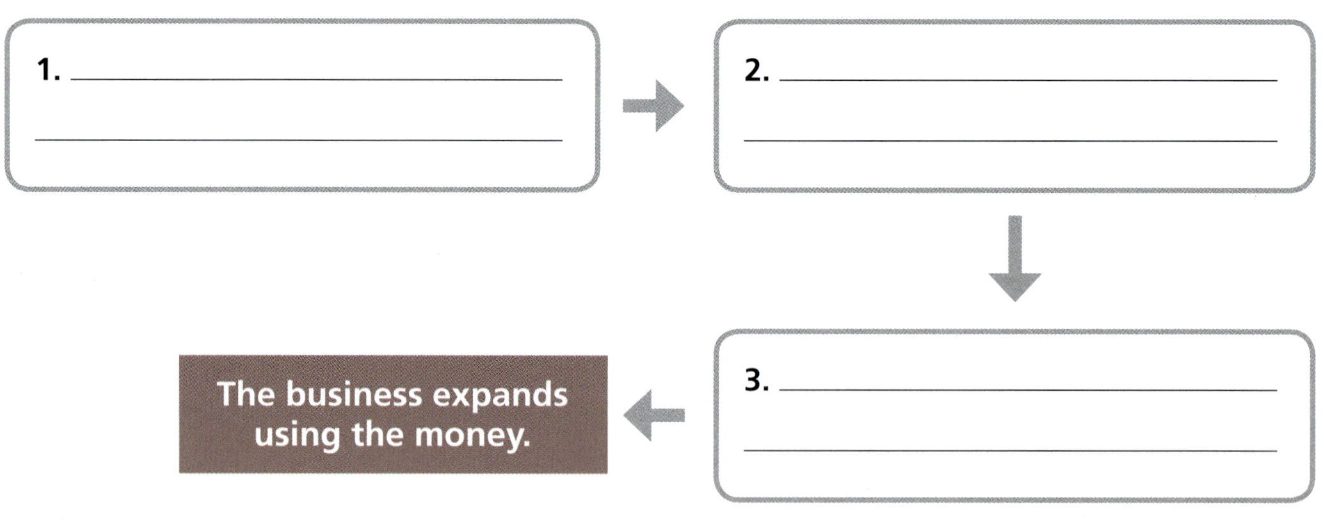

a. Investors buy stocks of the company.

b. The selling of the stocks raises money for the business.

c. A business decides to sell stocks of its company.

VOCABULARY

Choose the right word to complete each sentence. There are two extra words.

owns	cooperate	increase	profit	investor	hire	improve	stock

1. The business owner decided to ________________ two new workers.

2. My dad ________________ that ice cream shop.

3. I hope to sell this old painting for a lot of money and make a good ________________.

4. The restaurant needs to ________________ its space. It is always full.

5. The price of that company's ________________ went up today.

6. As a(n) ________________, you get to share the company's profits.

21st CENTURY SKILLS Critical Thinking Creativity Collaboration Communication

PROJECT Start Your Own Business

You learned how the stock market helps businesses make money. Now, let's start a business.

Step 1 Work in a small group. Think about a business you might want to start one day. Why do you want to start this business?

Sample We would like to start a(n) _company that makes chocolate_ because _we like to eat chocolate and we think lots of other kids do, too_.

We would like to start a(n) ________________________________

because ________________________________.

Step 2 Give your company a name and draw a picture of the things your business will sell.

Step 3 Make some stock certificates for your company on small pieces of paper.

Step 4 Show your class the picture you drew in Step 2 and try to sell your company's stocks. See which group sells the most stocks!

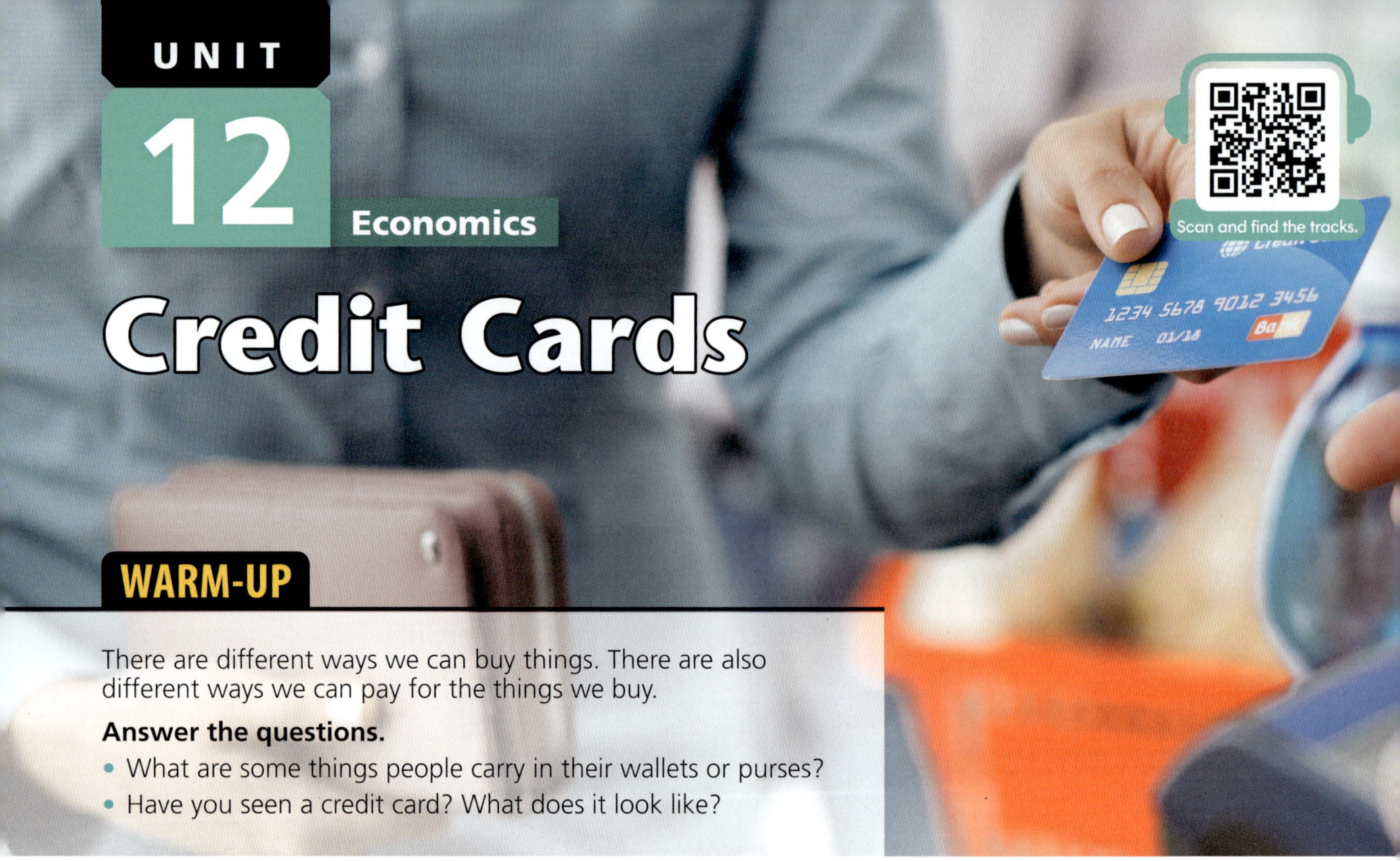

UNIT

12 Economics

Credit Cards

Scan and find the tracks.

WARM-UP

There are different ways we can buy things. There are also different ways we can pay for the things we buy.

Answer the questions.

- What are some things people carry in their wallets or purses?
- Have you seen a credit card? What does it look like?

NEW WORDS

Track 24

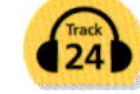

Listen and match the word with its meaning.

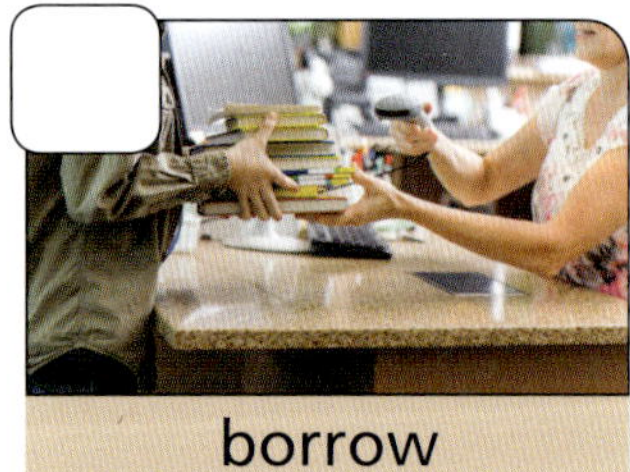

borrow

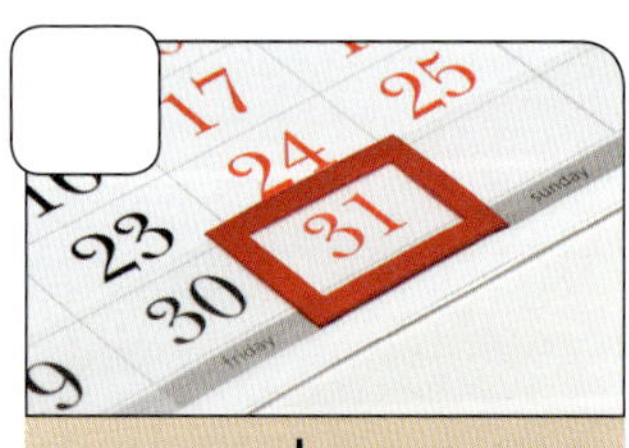

due

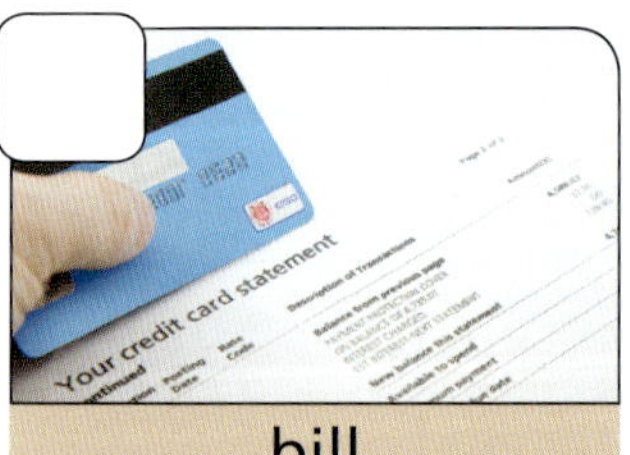

bill

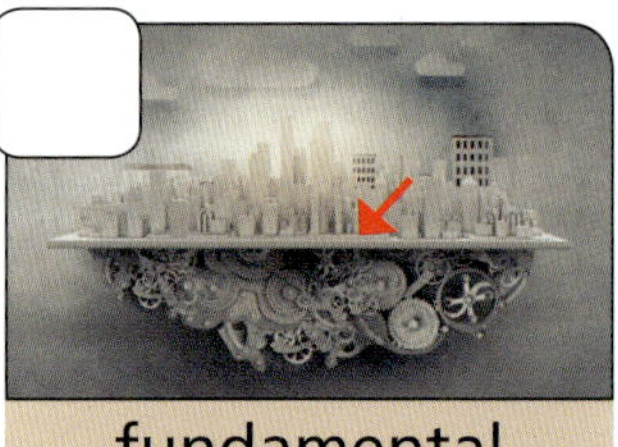

fundamental

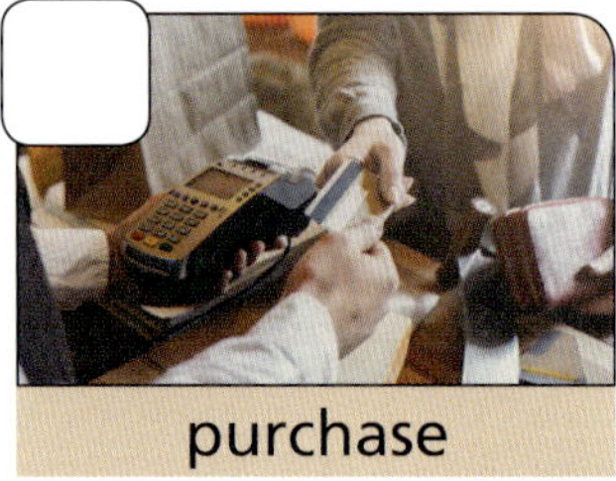

purchase

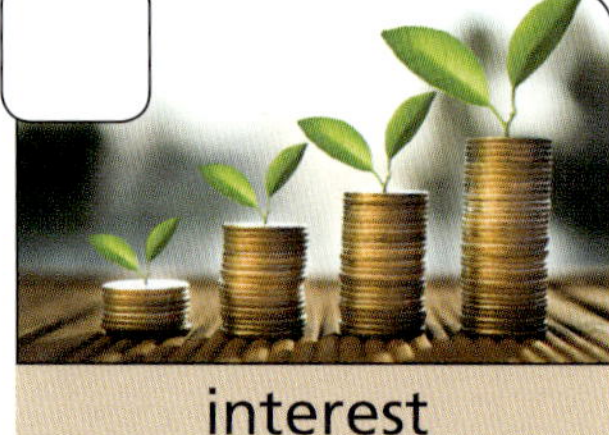

interest

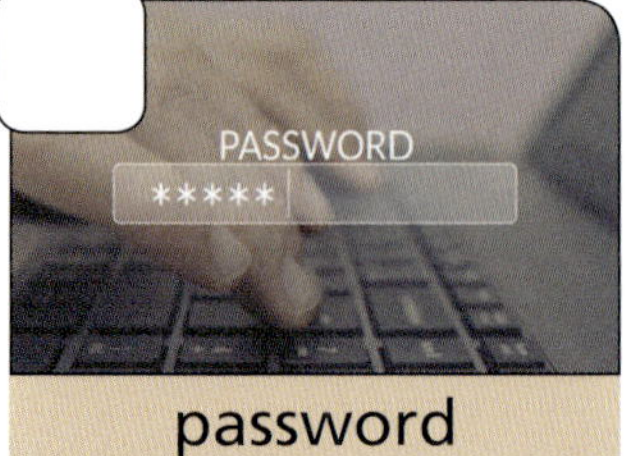

password

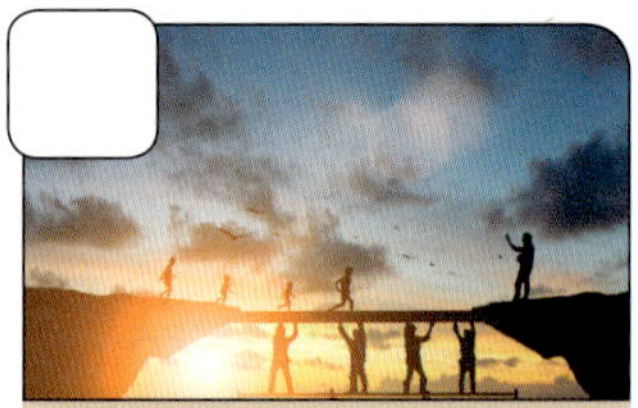

responsible

1. able to be trusted to do what is best
2. on the most important or simple level
3. required to be paid or returned by a certain date
4. to take and use something that belongs to someone else for a period of time before returning it
5. a secret set of numbers and letters that allows someone to use a computer system
6. extra money you pay if you borrow money
7. to buy
8. a note showing the amount of money that must be paid for something

READING 

Listen and read.

Credit Cards

Credit cards are small plastic cards that can be used to buy things. Only adults who earn money can get a credit card. It's important to understand how credit cards work. That way, people can be smart with their money.

Credit companies have money. When a person uses a credit card, they **borrow** the credit company's money. The amount of money that the credit company lends must be paid back by the person who owns the credit card. The amount that is **due** usually has to be paid in about thirty days. They can pay the whole amount when it is due, or pay in small amounts over time with **interest**.

There are two **fundamental** ways to use a credit card: offline and online. To pay offline, people put their card in a machine. When the card is used, the credit company pays the **bill**. To **purchase** things online, people type in their card number, **password**, and other information.

It's important to be **responsible** when using a credit card.

> Reading Time: _____m _____s / 169 words

READING COMPREHENSION

Choose the right answer.

1. What is the reading mainly about?
   a. How to buy goods easily
   b. How credit cards work
   c. Who can get credit cards
   d. How to get credit cards

2. A credit card company would probably give a credit card to __________.
   a. someone who has a good job
   b. someone who doesn't have a job
   c. a student who is in high school
   d. someone who doesn't have a lot of money

3. Which is NOT true according to the reading?
   a. People can use credit cards to buy things online.
   b. Credit cards are given to people who need to borrow money.
   c. You can pay back the credit card company within about one month.
   d. Credit card companies charge interest if you don't pay the whole bill.

READING SKILLS Summarizing

Complete the chart with the correct sentences.

Summary

Paragraph 1 →

Paragraph 2 →

Paragraph 3 →

Paragraph 4 →

a. There are two ways to use a credit card: in a store or on the internet.

b. Credit cards are one way to pay for things, and only people who earn money can get a card.

c. By using credit cards, people borrow the credit company's money and then pay it back with or without interest.

d. It is important to be smart and responsible when using a credit card.

VOCABULARY

Choose the right word to complete each sentence. There are two extra words.

| borrow | bill | fundamental | purchased | responsible | password | interest | due |

1. Have you paid for the things you ___________________?

2. I don't have enough money. Can I ___________________ five dollars from you?

3. The company will send a(n) ___________________ next month for what you bought.

4. The library book we borrowed is ___________________ tomorrow, so we should return it.

5. Keep your ___________________ secret. Don't give it to anyone.

6. If you don't pay on time, you will have to pay a lot of ___________________ and it will be expensive.

21st CENTURY SKILLS — Critical Thinking | Creativity | **Collaboration** | **Communication**

PROJECT Cash or Credit Card

You learned how credit cards work. Let's think more about credit cards, cash, and our own spending.

Step 1 Talk with a friend about whether you would prefer to pay cash for something or use a credit card. Why?

Sample For now, I would prefer to use _cash_ because _I think I would buy too much if I had a credit card_.

For now, I would prefer to use ___________________ because ___________________

___________________.

Step 2 With your friend, make a list of two things that each of you would buy if you did have a credit card. Talk together about why each of the things is important.

Sample I would like to buy _a new computer_ because _the one I have right now is very slow_.

I would like to buy ___________________ because ___________________.

Step 3 Show your list to the class, and find out which choices are the most popular.

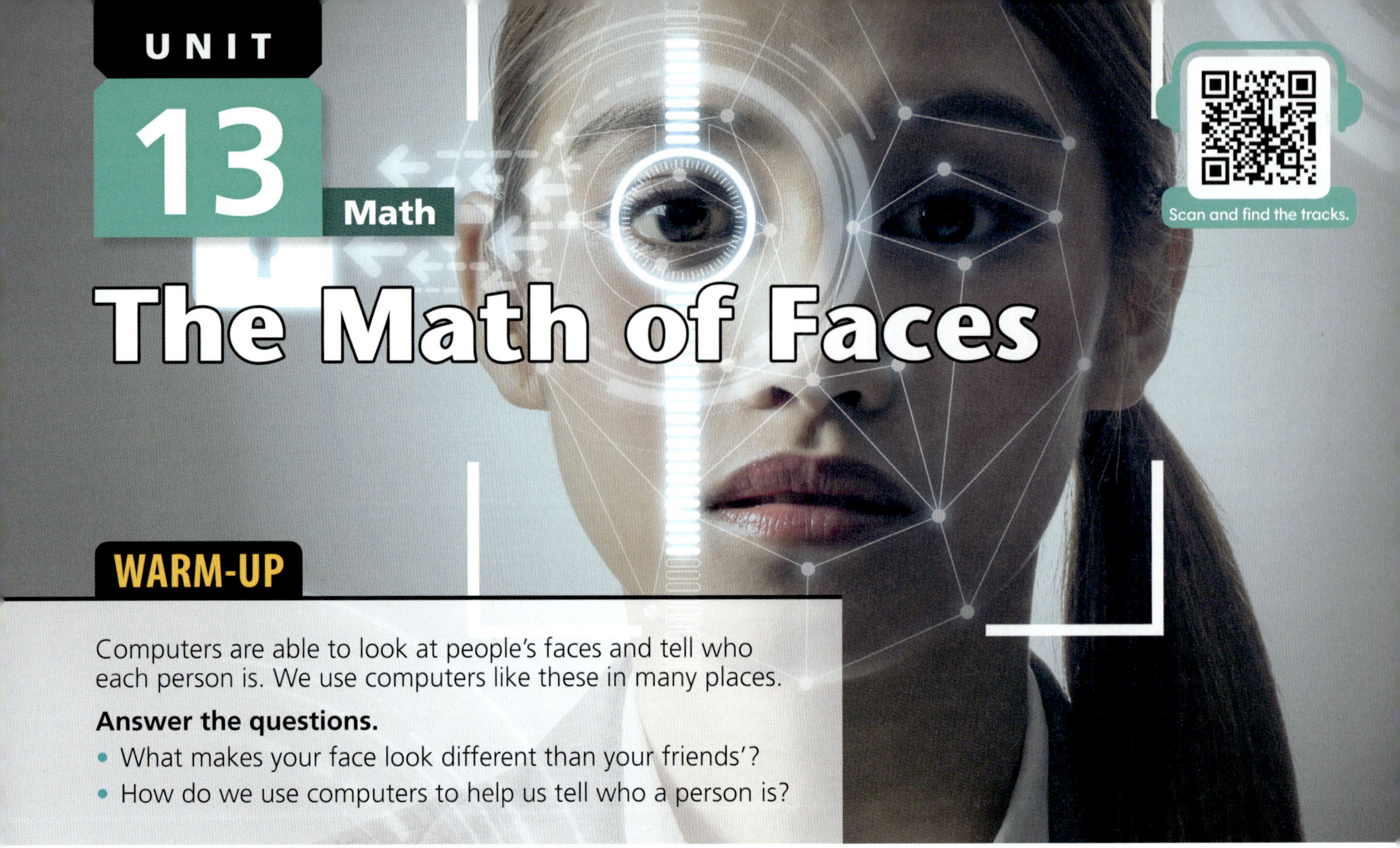

UNIT 13 Math

The Math of Faces

Scan and find the tracks.

WARM-UP

Computers are able to look at people's faces and tell who each person is. We use computers like these in many places.

Answer the questions.

- What makes your face look different than your friends'?
- How do we use computers to help us tell who a person is?

NEW WORDS

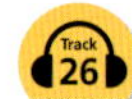

Track 26

Listen and match the word with its meaning.

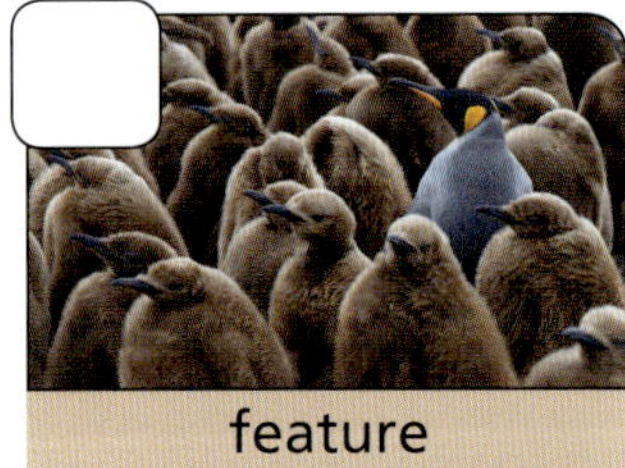

feature

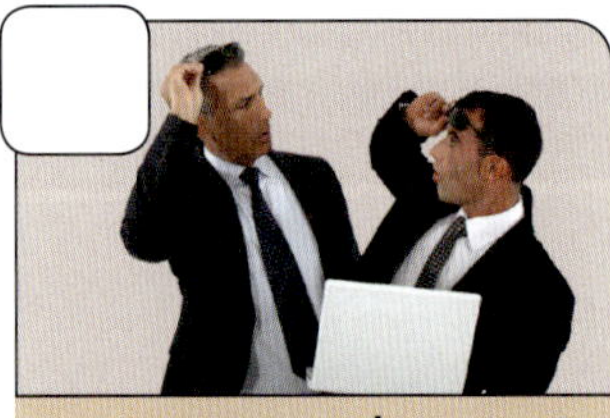

recognize

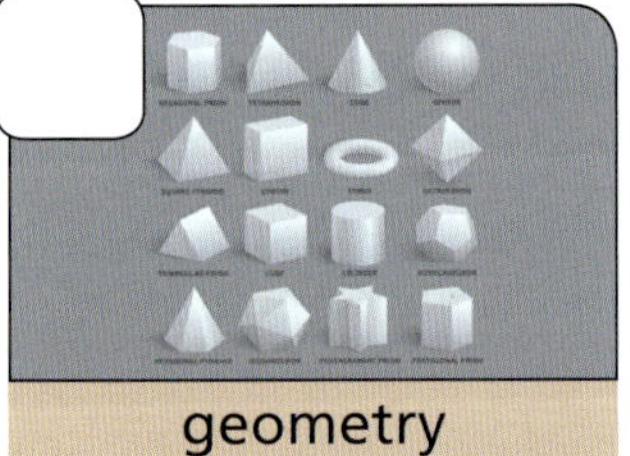

geometry

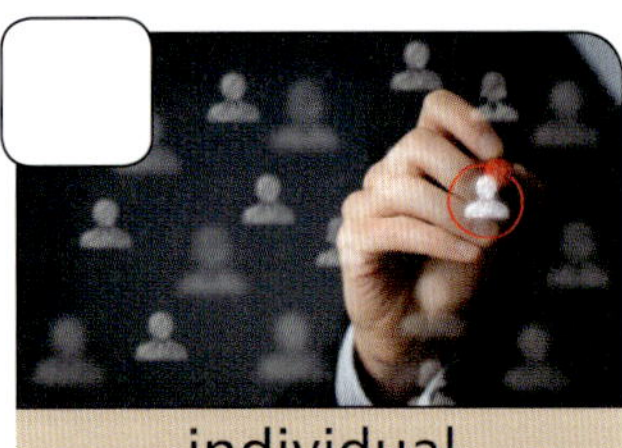

individual

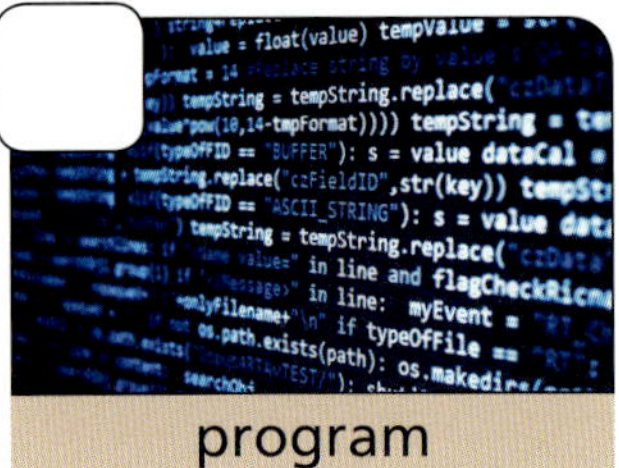

program

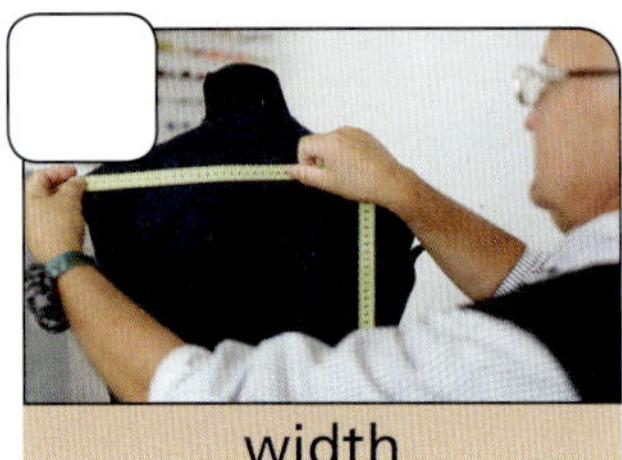

width

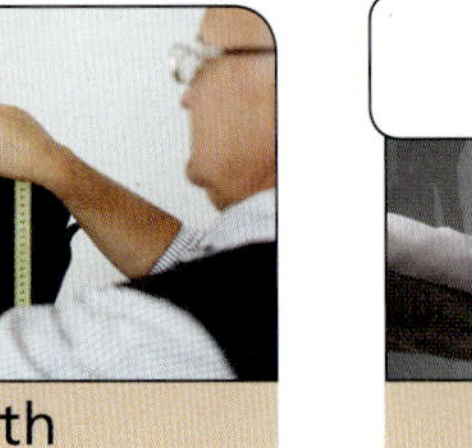

identify

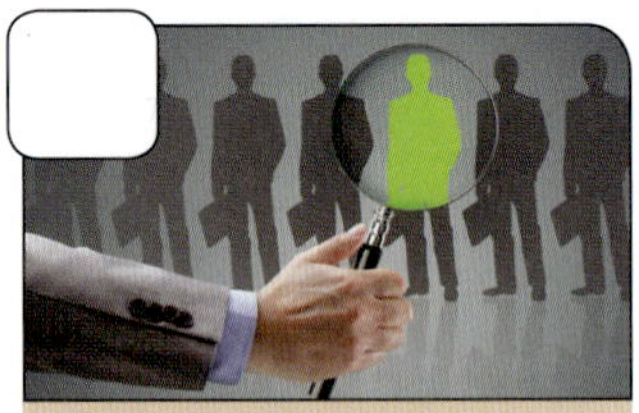

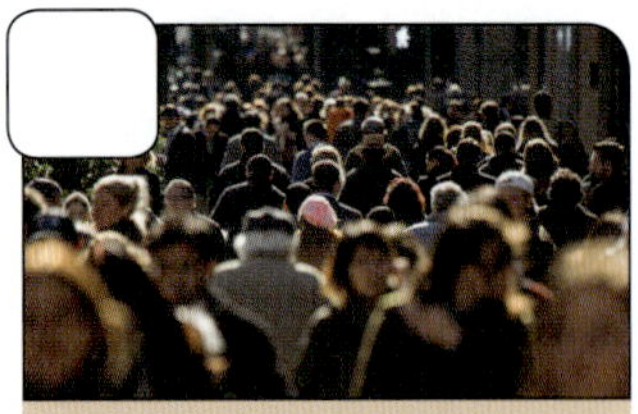

crowd

1. a large group of people
2. a type of math that deals with points, lines, angles, surfaces, shapes, and sizes
3. how wide something is
4. related to just one member or part of a larger group
5. a part of something that makes it special
6. to know someone or something
7. to pick out or select
8. a set of instructions that tells a computer what to do

Listen and read.

The Math of Faces

Almost everyone has different facial **features**. We see and analyze the space between a person's eyes, the shapes of their nose, and other different sizes and shapes on a person's face. Most people do this without really thinking about it. Computer **programs** can **recognize** these differences in people's faces, also. Actually, computers can do this much better than humans can. Facial recognition programs are used in many places and they are very helpful.

These computer programs record the **geometry** of the human face. Geometry is the type of math that studies shapes and sizes. Facial geometry measures many things. For example, it measures the exact distance between the eyes, the size of the eyes, the **width** of the mouth and nose, and more. Many measurements are taken. Together these measurements make a person's **individual** profile.

Facial recognition programs can **identify** people in a **crowd**. They are used for security at airports and in other important places. This technology also helps people to unlock their phones and even buy things.

Reading Time: _____ m _____ s / 169 words

VOCABULARY SKILLS

There are words that can be both nouns and verbs.

- **face** *n.* the front part of the head
  v. to be positioned with the face toward
- **hand** *n.* the body part at the end of the arm
  v. to give
- **answer** *n.* something that you say or write to a question
  v. to say or write something to a question
- **work** *n.* a job or activity
  v. to do a job

READING SKILLS

Main Idea & Details

The main idea of a paragraph is what it is mostly about. Details, explanations, and examples can help readers find the main idea.

- What is paragraph 2 mostly about?
  ____

- What is paragraph 3 mostly about?
  ____

READING COMPREHENSION

Choose the right answer.

1. What is the reading mainly about?

    a. How computer programs work

    b. How companies can use crowds

    c. Why faces are all different

    d. How computers can recognize faces

2. According to the reading, what is geometry?

    a. A computer program

    b. A kind of mathematics

    c. A measurement of width

    d. A technology people use

3. Which is NOT true according to the reading?

    a. Facial geometry measures only eye size.

    b. Computers can recognize people's faces.

    c. Different features of the face are measured to make a profile.

    d. A facial recognition program can pick out one person in a crowd.

READING SKILLS   Main Idea & Details

Complete the chart with the correct information.

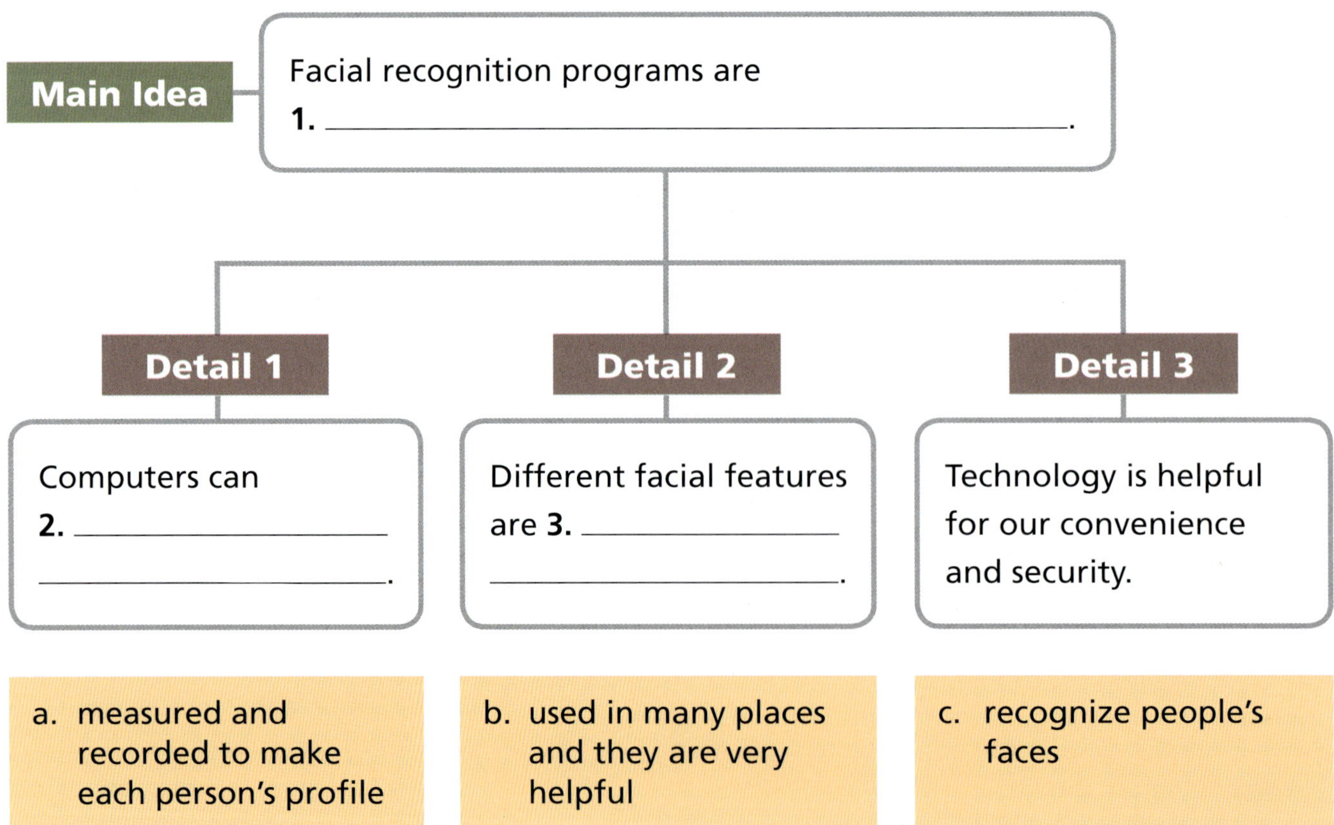

VOCABULARY

Choose the right word to complete each sentence. There are two extra words.

| width   features   recognized   geometry   program   individual   identify   crowds |

1. We are learning ___________________ in math class now.
2. Red hair and green eyes are some unique ___________________ I have.
3. Each ___________________ person has their own card with their picture on it.
4. Measure the ___________________ of the table to see if it can go through the door.
5. The new computer ___________________ understands what I say.
6. He doesn't like ___________________ and usually stays away when there are lots of people.

21st CENTURY SKILLS   Critical Thinking   Creativity   Collaboration   Communication

PROJECT Facial Features

You learned that computers use facial geometry to recognize faces. Now, let's describe people's facial features.

Step 1   Look at the pictures of the people below. How would you describe their features?

Jane / eyes   Ben / nose   Greg / mouth

Sample   I see that _Jane has very big eyes_.

I see that ____.

I see that ____.

Step 2   Draw a picture of a face. Then describe the face to a friend so they can draw a picture. Compare your pictures.

Sample   The face has _small eyes and a large nose_. It also has _a wide mouth_.

The face has ____.

It also has ____.

Cooking with Math

WARM-UP

Students sometimes wonder when they will use the math they learn in the classroom in their real life. We can use math in many places, including at home when we cook.

Answer the questions.

- What is one way you use math in your real life?
- How do you think we can use math while cooking food?

NEW WORDS (Track 28)

Listen and match the word with its meaning.

aid	kitchen	vanilla	double

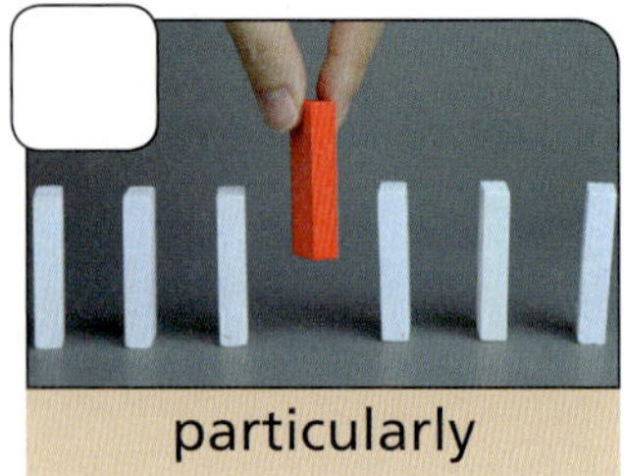   

particularly	calculation	culinary	tricky

1. difficult to do or deal with
2. especially
3. to make or become twice as much
4. to give help
5. a room where food is cooked
6. a food product that is made from a bean and used to add a flavor to food
7. related to cooking
8. something you work out using math

Cooking with Math

Using math can **aid** us in real life, **particularly** in the **kitchen**.

Let's say you want to make cookies for twenty people. The cookie recipe you have only makes ten cookies. If you know how to add fractions, you can follow this recipe and make twenty cookies.

The recipe says you need 1 cup of flour, 1/2 cup of sugar, 1/2 cup of butter, 3/4 cup of chocolate chips, 1 spoon of **vanilla**, 1/2 spoon of baking powder, and 1 egg. Add fractions to **double** the recipe.

Start with the whole numbers: $1 + 1 = 2$. So you need 2 cups of flour, 2 eggs, and 2 spoons of vanilla.

Next are the 1/2 fractions: $1/2 + 1/2 = 2/2$, and $2/2 = 1$. So you need 1 cup of sugar, 1 cup of butter, and 1 spoon of baking powder.

Finally, 3/4 cup of chocolate chips: $3/4 + 3/4 = 6/4$, and $6/4 = 1\,2/4$. $2/4 = 1/2$, so you'd need $1\tfrac{1}{2}$ cups of chocolate chips.

Adding fractions can help with those **tricky culinary calculations**.

Reading Time: ______m ______s / 169 words

READING COMPREHENSION

Choose the right answer.

1. What is the reading mainly about?

    a. How to cook food   b. How to earn money

    c. How to buy food for lunch   d. How to use fractions to measure things

2. How much sugar is needed to make cookies for twenty people?

    a. ½ cup   b. 1 cup

    c. ½ spoon   d. 1 spoon

3. Which is NOT true according to the reading?

    a. Adding fractions can help with cooking.

    b. You can make cookies for twenty people.

    c. You need one egg to cook for ten people.

    d. You need ½ cup of chocolate chips to make cookies for twenty people.

READING SKILLS Sequencing

Complete the chart with the correct information.

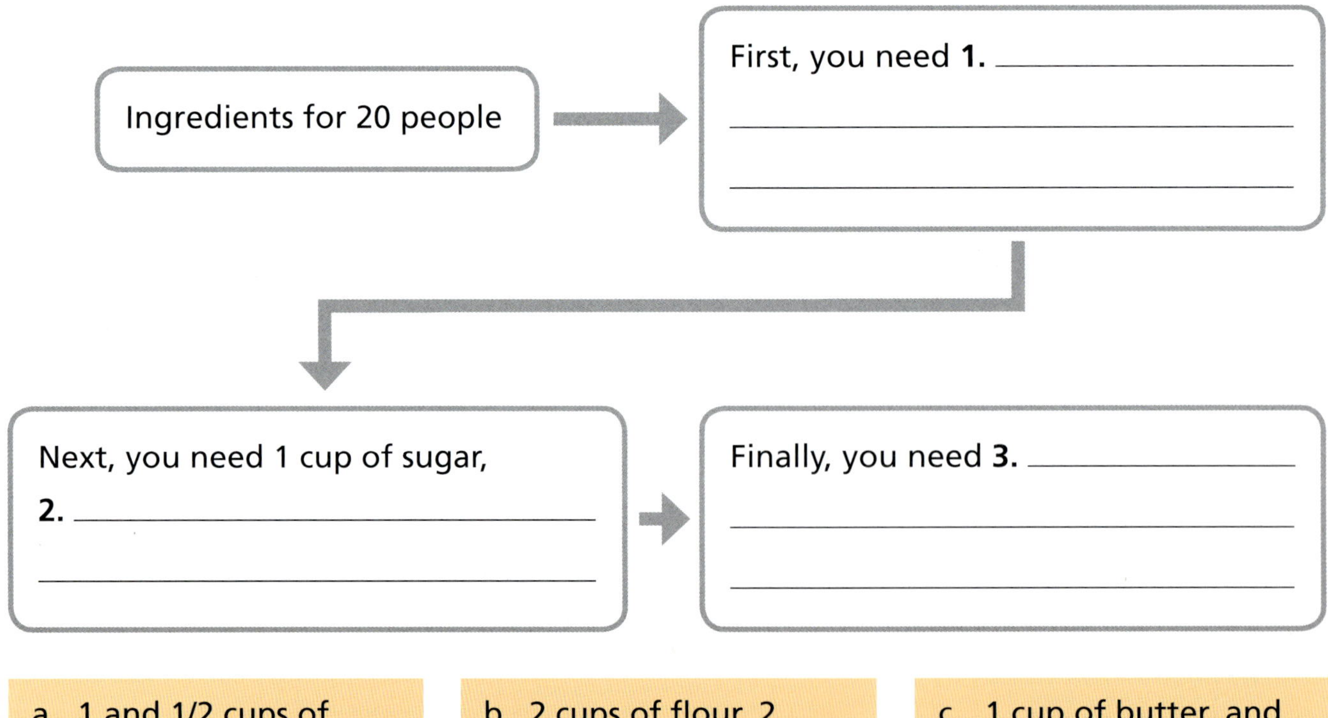

VOCABULARY

Choose the right word to complete each sentence. There are two extra words.

aid	kitchen	tricky	vanilla	double	particularly	calculation	culinary

1. We cook breakfast, lunch, and dinner in the _______________.
2. My two favorite flavors of ice cream are chocolate and _______________ flavored ice cream.
3. Your donation will _______________ flood victims
4. He is _______________ good at solving tricky problems.
5. The head chef of this restaurant graduated from the best _______________ school in the city.
6. The boy is struggling with the _______________ question.

21st CENTURY SKILLS — Critical Thinking · Creativity · Collaboration · Communication

PROJECT Using Fractions

You learned about using fractions in cooking. Now, let's talk about other things that can be shown in fractions.

Step 1 Look at the pictures. How can you write about how much or how many there are?

Pizza (left on the plate) | Children (girls or boy) | Fish (in the bowl or out of the bowl)

Sample _1/2 of the pizza_ (is / are) _left on the plate_.

_______________ (is / are) _______________.

_______________ (is / are) _______________.

Step 2 Work with a friend. Think about the students in your class. How many boys and girls are there? How can you write the number of girls and boys as a fraction?

Sample There are _twelve boys and eight girls_ in my class. This means _12/20 of my class are boys and 8/20 of my class are girls_.

There are _______________ in my class. This means

_______________.

Measurement Systems

WARM-UP

Just as people from different cultures speak different languages, they use different systems to measure things like length, weight, and other things.

Answer the questions.
- What are different ways to show how tall something is?
- What could happen if your numbers about how tall you are were wrong?

NEW WORDS 

Listen and match the word with its meaning.

currently

widely

pound

mile

trouble

agency

unfortunately

fail

1. problems
2. at the present time; now
3. a measurement of weight in the imperial system
4. used to say that something is sad or has bad luck
5. a measurement of distance in the imperial system
6. to do badly or not succeed
7. a part of the government that is responsible for doing a particular job
8. very much or by a lot of people

Listen and read.

Measurement Systems

Today, there are two **widely** used systems of measurement around the world. They are the metric system and the imperial system. The imperial system is older, and long ago it was the most widely used system. But later the metric system was introduced. **Currently**, most of the world uses that system. It uses measurements like kilometers and kilograms. However, some countries continue to use the imperial system. It uses measurements like **miles** and **pounds**. America is one of those countries.

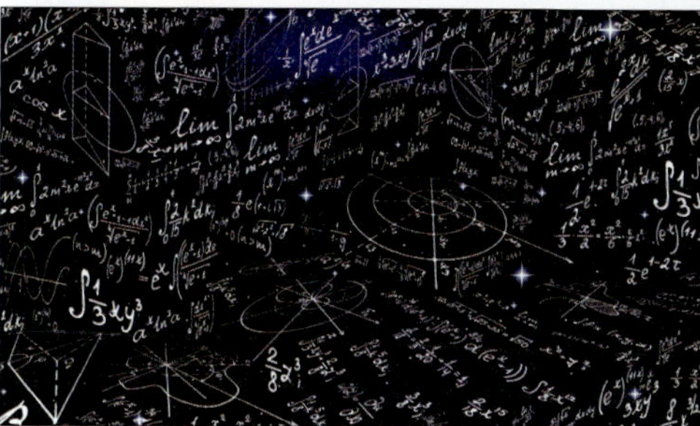

Unfortunately, this caused **trouble** for the American space **agency**, NASA. In 1998, NASA sent a spaceship to Mars on a mission. While building the spaceship, NASA used the metric system. This made working with other countries easier. But one of the American companies NASA worked with didn't consider this. That company made an important computer program for the spaceship. They used imperial measurements, but all of the other programs and calculations used metric measurements. As a result, the ship crashed on September 23rd, 1999, and the mission **failed**.

Reading Time: _____ m _____ s / 168 words

VOCABULARY SKILLS

Knowing the difference between metric and imperial measurements can be very helpful.

- 1 **pound**: 0.454 kg (kilograms)
- 1 **inch**: 2.54 cm (centimeters)
- 1 **mile**: 1.609 km (kilometers)

READING SKILLS

Cause & Effect

An effect is something that happens. The cause is why or how that thing happened.

- What caused the mission to fail? <u>Underline</u> the sentence in the reading.

READING COMPREHENSION

Choose the right answer.

1. What is the reading mainly about?
   a. How to build a spaceship
   b. How to measure Mars
   c. How to use imperial measurements
   d. How different measurements can cause problems

2. Who made the mistake that caused the problem?
   a. America
   b. Other countries
   c. NASA
   d. A company

3. Which is NOT true according to the reading?
   a. A computer that used imperial measurements caused the mission to fail.
   b. The spaceship was built using different measurement systems.
   c. The spaceship crashed because of mistakes in measurement.
   d. NASA worked with a company that used imperial measurements.

READING SKILLS Cause & Effect

Complete the chart with the correct sentences.

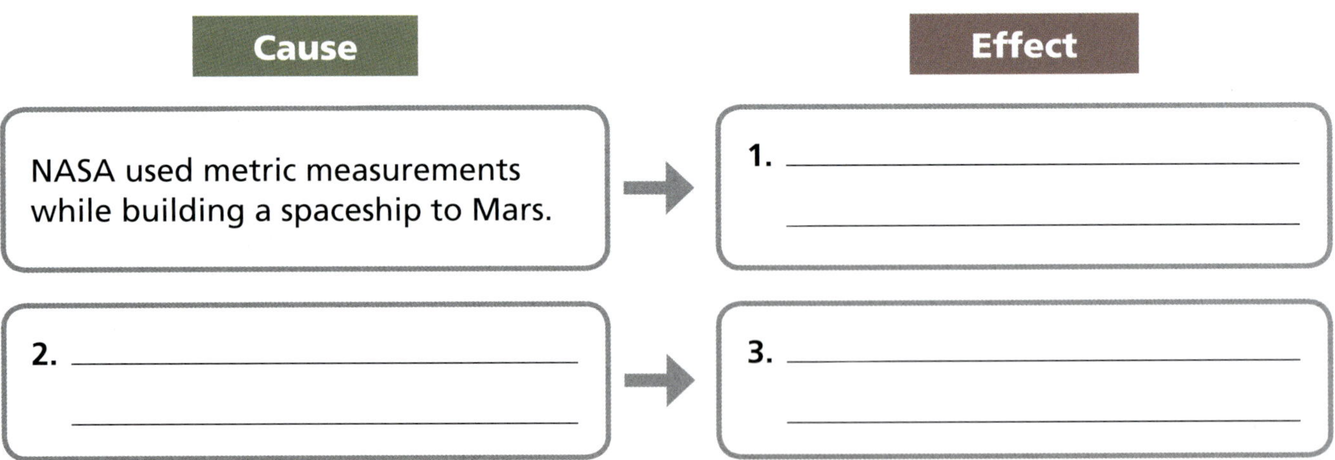

a. The spaceship crashed and the mission failed.

b. It was easier to work with other countries participating in the project.

c. One computer program used imperial measurements, but all others used the metric system.

VOCABULARY

Choose the right word to complete each sentence. There are two extra words.

| currently | widely | pounds | mile | trouble | unfortunately | agency | fail |

1. I walked a(n) ______________ to the park, but it didn't take long.

2. My father weighs about 85 kilograms, or about 187 ______________.

3. I am not ______________ exercising because I hurt my leg.

4. The Russian space ______________ sent the first woman into space.

5. You will ______________ your exams if you do not try harder.

6. It is ______________ known that the company is in trouble.

21st CENTURY SKILLS — Critical Thinking · Creativity · Collaboration · Communication

PROJECT Using Different Measurements

You learned that problems can happen when people use different systems to measure something. Let's look at how the systems are different.

Step 1 Think about something to measure in metric units. What will you measure? What unit will you use?

Sample I am going to measure _the distance from my home to my school_. I will use _kilometers_.

I am going to measure ____.

I will use ____.

Step 2 Write down your measurement.

Sample _My school is three kilometers away from my home._

____

Step 3 Change the measurement to imperial units. How are the numbers different? What might happen if the units were mixed up? Share with a friend.

Measuring Big Animals in the Wild

WARM-UP

Scientists study animals to get important information. Some animals are easy to measure, but others can be quite difficult.

Answer the questions.
- How do you measure things? What can you use to measure things?
- Do you think it is easy to measure large animals? Why or why not?

NEW WORDS (Track 32)

Listen and match the word or phrase with its meaning.

creative

collect

approximate

manual

tool

figure out

estimate

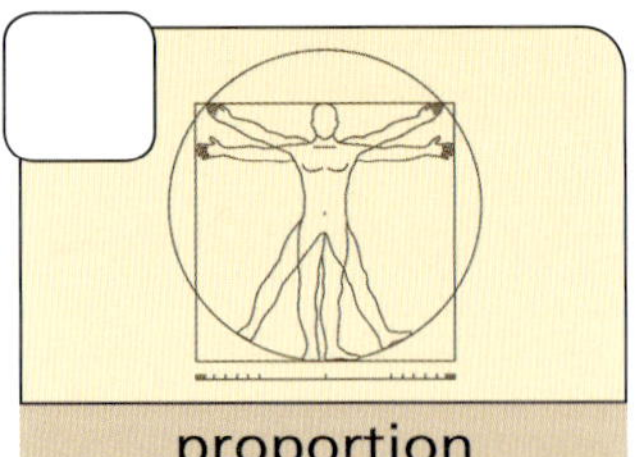
proportion

1. something you use to help you do work
2. to bring things together
3. the size and shape of something
4. a best guess of the size, value, amount, etc.
5. original or clever
6. close in value or amount but not exact
7. doing something by hand, without electricity
8. to understand or solve something

Listen and read.

Measuring Big Animals in the Wild

Some things are easy to measure. Just use a simple tool, and read the measurement. But a big animal, like a whale in the ocean, can't be measured easily. Scientists need to find creative ways to use math to measure these big animals.

To measure whales, scientists usually start by studying dead ones. Sometimes, the body of a dead whale washes up on a beach. Scientists do manual measurements of these animals. To do this, scientists use <u>tools</u> like a measuring tape or a scale.

After measuring many dead whales and collecting a lot of information, scientists can figure out the approximate proportions of a whale. Scientists use this information to know about the size of living whales.

They also take pictures of animals they want to study. They take as many pictures as they can. They try to collect as much information as they can about the animal. Then they make an estimate of the length and weight of the animal.

Scientists use math creatively to measure big animals.

> Reading Time: _____ m _____ s / 170 words

VOCABULARY SKILLS

A word with the suffix **-ist** means a person who works with or studies the thing referred to by that word.

science+ist → scient**ist**

- art**ist**: someone who creates art
- pian**ist**: someone who plays the piano
- tour**ist**: someone who tours around a new place
- journal**ist**: someone who reports news for a journal or newspaper

READING SKILLS

Sequencing

Sequencing helps you understand the order in which events take place in a reading.

- What happens before scientists can take manual measurements of a whale?

READING COMPREHENSION

Choose the right answer.

1. What is the reading mainly about?
   - a. How to use measuring tools
   - b. How to measure large animals
   - c. How to understand whales
   - d. How to take photographs of animals

2. What does the word <u>tools</u> in line 9 mean in the reading?
   - a. estimates of length and weight
   - b. dead animals
   - c. things used to measure
   - d. places scientists go to study animals

3. Which is NOT true according to the reading?
   - a. Dead whales sometimes wash up on the beach.
   - b. Scientists make estimates of the size of dead animals.
   - c. Scientists can more easily measure a dead animal.
   - d. Scientists use tools to measure dead animals by hand.

READING SKILLS Sequencing

Complete the chart with the correct information.

First, scientists study **1.** ___________________________________

___________________________________.

↓

After that, **2.** ___________________________________

___________________________________.

↓

Then, **3.** ___________________________________

___________________________________.

- a. they make an estimate of the length and weight of the living animals
- b. they take manual measurements of the dead animals
- c. dead animals that have washed up on shore

VOCABULARY

Choose the right word or phrase to complete each sentence. There are two extra words.

figure out   collects   creative   estimate   approximate   manual   tool   proportions

1. He is very ___________________ and easily thinks of new ideas.

2. The teacher ___________________ our homework to check them.

3. It was hard to count them all, so he made a(n) ___________________ of the number of birds in the park.

4. I know my dog's ___________________ age but not the exact age.

5. The carpet doesn't fit in the room because it has the wrong ___________________.

6. My dad bought a new ___________________ to cut wood.

PROJECT Other Ways to Measure

You learned how scientists can measure large animals in the wild. Now, let's think about some other ways to take measurements.

Step 1 Look at the pictures. Think about some creative ways you can measure the length of these things.

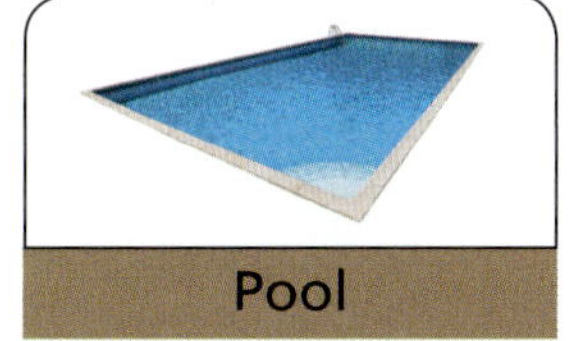

Pool

Classroom

School bus

Sample I can _use my feet to measure the length of the classroom_.

I can ____.

I can ____.

Step 2 Think about one other large thing to measure. What is the best way to measure it? What tool(s) will you need? How can you measure with that tool? Share what you think with your class.

Sample I can use a _measuring tape_ to measure _my house_. I can _ask a friend to help me by holding one end of the measuring tape_. Then I can _run to the other end of the house with the measuring tape to see how long it is_.

Reading Speed Chart

Time how long it takes you to read each passage. Then use the formula in the box to find your words per minute (WPM) score. Color in the boxes to see how you improve.

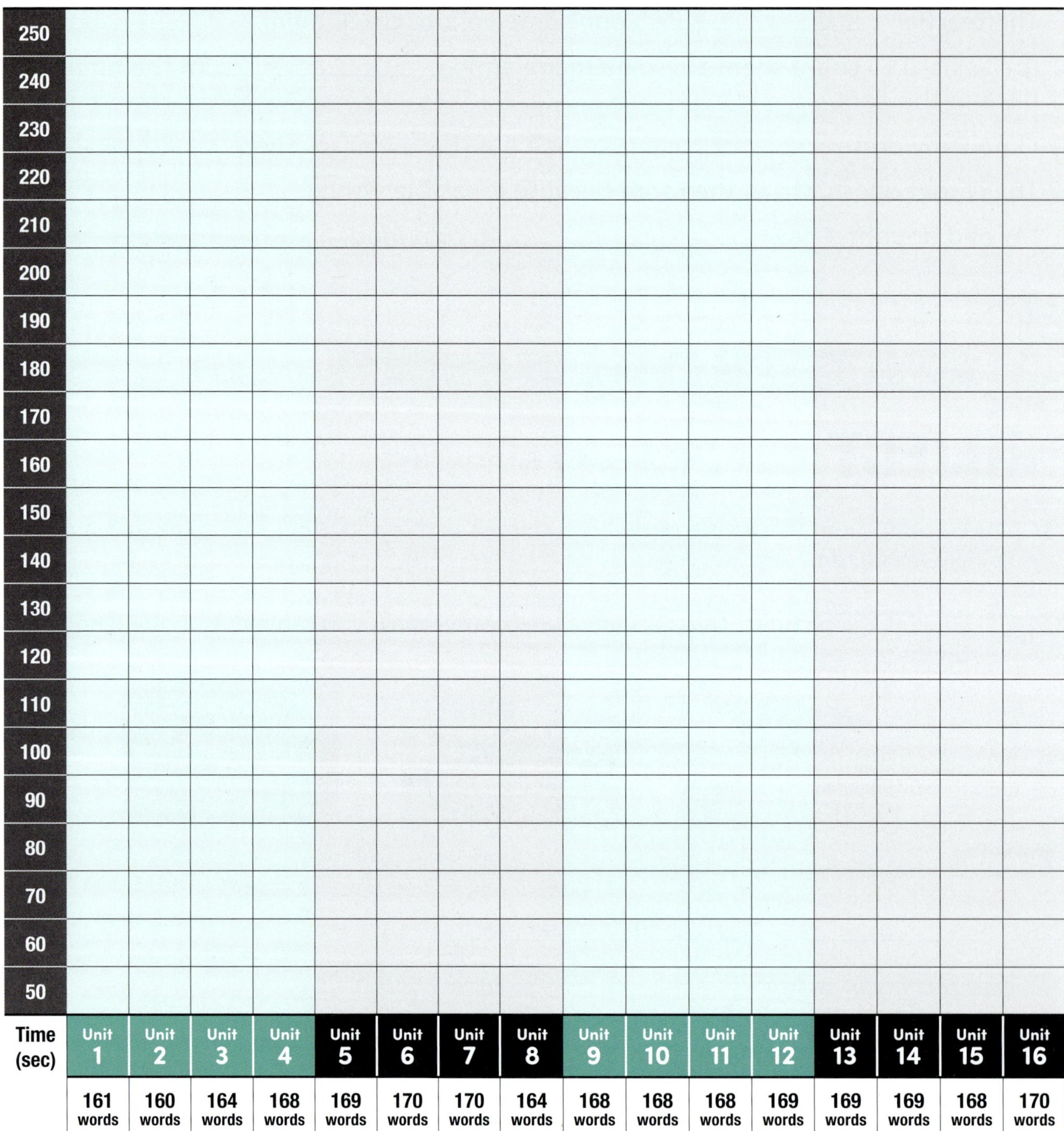

Unit 1	Unit 2	Unit 3	Unit 4	Unit 5	Unit 6	Unit 7	Unit 8	Unit 9	Unit 10	Unit 11	Unit 12	Unit 13	Unit 14	Unit 15	Unit 16
161 words	160 words	164 words	168 words	169 words	170 words	170 words	164 words	168 words	168 words	168 words	169 words	169 words	169 words	168 words	170 words

Formula

(Word Count ÷ Reading Time in Seconds) X 60 = ______________ WPM score

READING FUTURE

CHANGE

Workbook

Starter
Dream
Discover
Develop
Connect
Change
Create

Susan Ludwig · Kelli Ripatti
Tamara Wilburn · Lucas Foster

2

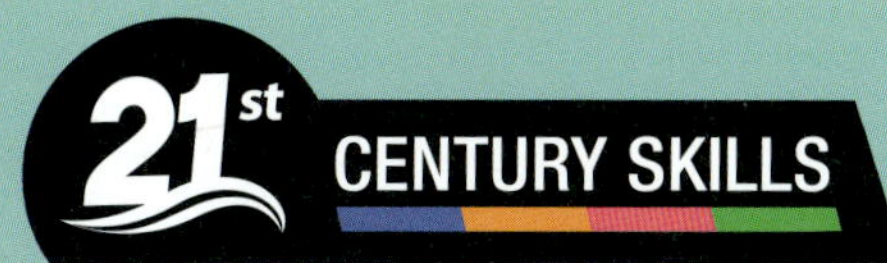

READING FUTURE

CHANGE

Workbook

2

Susan Ludwig · Kelli Ripatti
Tamara Wilburn · Lucas Foster

Table of Contents

Artificial Limbs

VOCABULARY CHECK

Complete the puzzle.

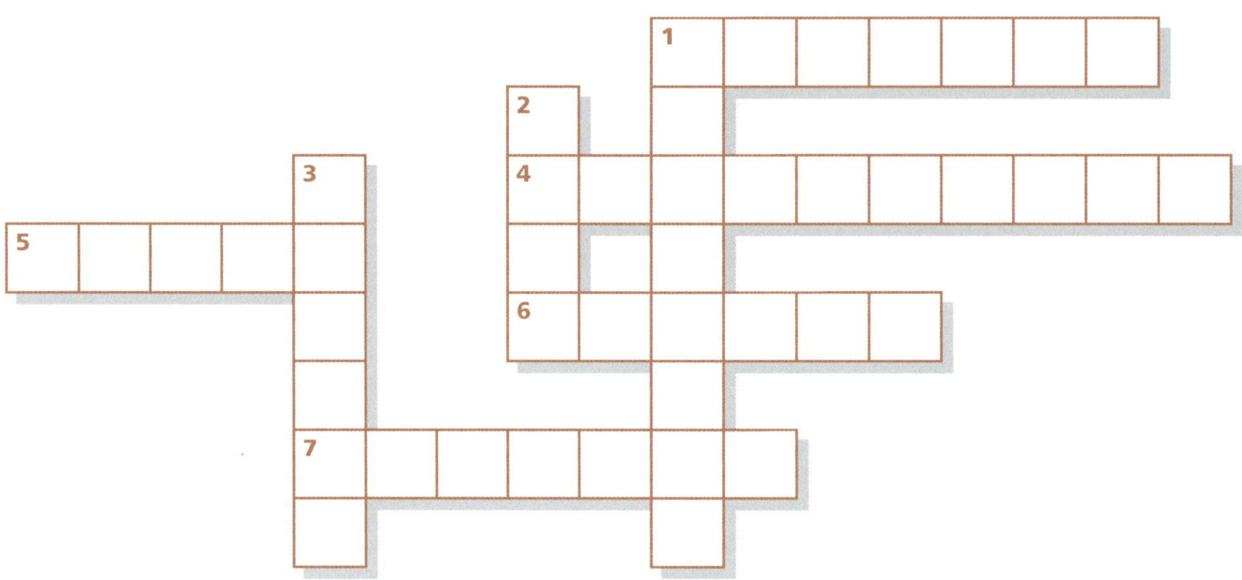

Across →

1. to take the place of something that was there before
4. not natural; made by people
5. not heavy
6. to make longer
7. to do something as a reaction to something else that has happened or been done

Down ↓

1. moving around a point in the center
2. not real or true
3. a series of steps that go from one level or floor to another

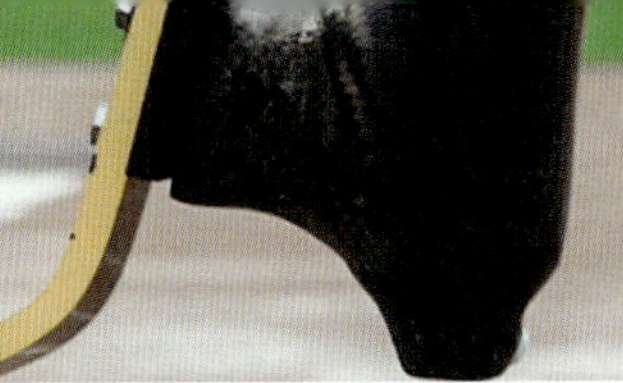

COMPREHENSION CHECK

Choose and write the right answer for each question.

Wires for computers	Metal hooks and wood
Help people feel objects	Open and close the fingers
Rotating knees that bend and extend	Computer chips

1. What things were used as artificial limbs in the past?

   ____

2. What can electronic hands do today?

   ____

3. What allows users to climb stairs and ride bikes?

   ____

4. What do scientists want to put into people's brains to help them use artificial limbs?

   ____

SUMMARY

Complete the summary. Not all the words will be used.

artificial	replace	light	respond
extend	fake	rotating	stairs

Humans and machines make ❶ _______________ limbs to ❷ _______________ missing limbs. Artificial limbs are ❸ _______________ arms and legs. In the past, artificial limbs were ugly and difficult to use. Today, artificial limbs are more like natural limbs. They are ❹ _______________ and have moving parts. Some electronic artificial hands ❺ _______________ to movements in the muscles. Artificial legs have ❻ _______________ knees that bend and ❼ _______________. In the future, thoughts will control artificial limbs. Scientists are already working on computer chips that will allow users to use their brain to move their artificial limbs.

Winners Wear Red

VOCABULARY CHECK

Complete the puzzle.

Across →

3. a result
4. a person or group that you are playing against in a contest
6. in a way that always happens without having to try to make it happen
7. to have an effect on someone or something
8. a special kind of clothing that is worn by all the members of a group

Down ↓

1. a contest in which people try to win by being better, faster, etc., than others
2. happening a short time ago
5. just; only

COMPREHENSION CHECK

Choose and write the right answer for each question.

England	Wearing favorite color	Wearing red color
Recently	Long time ago	The largest sports competitions

1. What can help athletes?

____

2. Which country are the researchers from?

____

3. When did the study happen?

____

4. Where did the researchers go for their study?

____

SUMMARY

Complete the summary. Not all the words will be used.

recent	uniform	outcome	competitions
opponents	simply	influence	automatically

Some athletes choose a(n) **1** _________________ that is their favorite color. However, if you're an athlete you should try to wear red. A(n) **2** _________________ study showed that wearing red can help athletes. The researchers went to some of the largest sports **3** _________________ in the world. They wanted to know if changing the uniform color would change the **4** _________________ of the match. The results showed that athletes who wore red usually beat their **5** _________________ who wore other colors. Remember you cannot put on a red shirt and expect to **6** _________________ win every match. There are other things that **7** _________________ the outcome of a match, too.

VOCABULARY CHECK

Complete the puzzle.

Across →

3. without sound
4. to make something smaller or less
5. done by many people; usual
6. the building of things like houses
7. the condition of the body

Down ↓

1. being important or possibly dangerous
2. all the cars, trucks, etc., driving on a road
4. to learn; to understand

COMPREHENSION CHECK

Choose and write the right answer for each question.

Sound that has a bad effect on humans	It affects our health.
Planes	It's not a big problem.
Traffic	By lowering the volume of the TV

1. What is noise pollution?

____

2. Where does most noise pollution come from?

____

3. Why do we need to care about noise pollution?

____

4. How can we reduce the noise we make?

____

SUMMARY

Complete the summary. Not all the words will be used.

realize	common	serious	reduce
health	construction	traffic	silent

Some people may not **1** _______________ that their houses are full of noise pollution. One of the most **2** _______________ forms of pollution is noise pollution. This is machine-made sound that has a bad effect on human **3** _______________. Most noise pollution comes from **4** _______________, but planes, **5** _______________, even loud TVs add to the problem. Noise pollution can cause hearing problems and stress. Over time, stress can cause other **6** _______________ problems in our bodies. People should try to **7** _______________ the noise they make so that they can improve their own health.

Understanding the Heart

VOCABULARY CHECK

Find the words in the puzzle. Then, fill in the blanks.

A	C	N	V	S	R	Z	F	G	R
C	H	E	I	I	R	N	X	D	U
J	A	C	T	F	T	S	O	P	Z
S	M	E	A	D	J	A	N	U	I
O	B	S	M	I	U	A	L	M	E
E	E	S	I	R	G	J	D	P	M
P	R	A	N	R	L	U	Y	K	A
H	X	R	O	X	Y	G	E	N	F
X	F	Y	Q	U	M	F	X	B	W
Y	X	E	M	P	T	Y	A	O	J

1. an important part inside your body: _______________________

2. so important that you must do it or have it; absolutely needed: _______________________

3. needed to stay alive or for something to be done: _______________________

4. a closed space inside something: _______________________

5. to make liquid or gas flow: _______________________

6. to remove all of something from something else: _______________________

7. a natural thing that is usually in food and that helps your body to be healthy: _______________________

8. a chemical that is found in the air, that has no color, taste, or smell, and that is needed for life: _______________________

COMPREHENSION CHECK

Choose and write the right answer for each question.

Tubes that blood is carried through	Tubes in which blood stays	Blood
A transportation system	Veins	Arteries

1. What are the chambers of heart filled with?

    ____

2. What are blood vessels?

    ____

3. Which vessels carry blood away from the heart?

    ____

4. What is blood like?

    ____

SUMMARY

Complete the summary. Not all the words will be used.

necessary	organs	empties	oxygen
heart	chambers	pumps	vitamins

The heart is one of the five vital **1** _______________ in the human body. These organs, such as the heart, are **2** _______________ for humans to stay alive. Inside the heart, there are four parts called **3** _______________. The heart beats and fills the chambers with blood. Then the heart **4** _______________ the chambers. It **5** _______________ blood from the chambers through the body. Blood carries many important things through the body, such as **6** _______________ and oxygen. The human heart pumps 7,500 liters of blood through your body every day. It works hard, so keep your **7** _______________ healthy!

Hypertext Literature

VOCABULARY CHECK

Complete the puzzle.

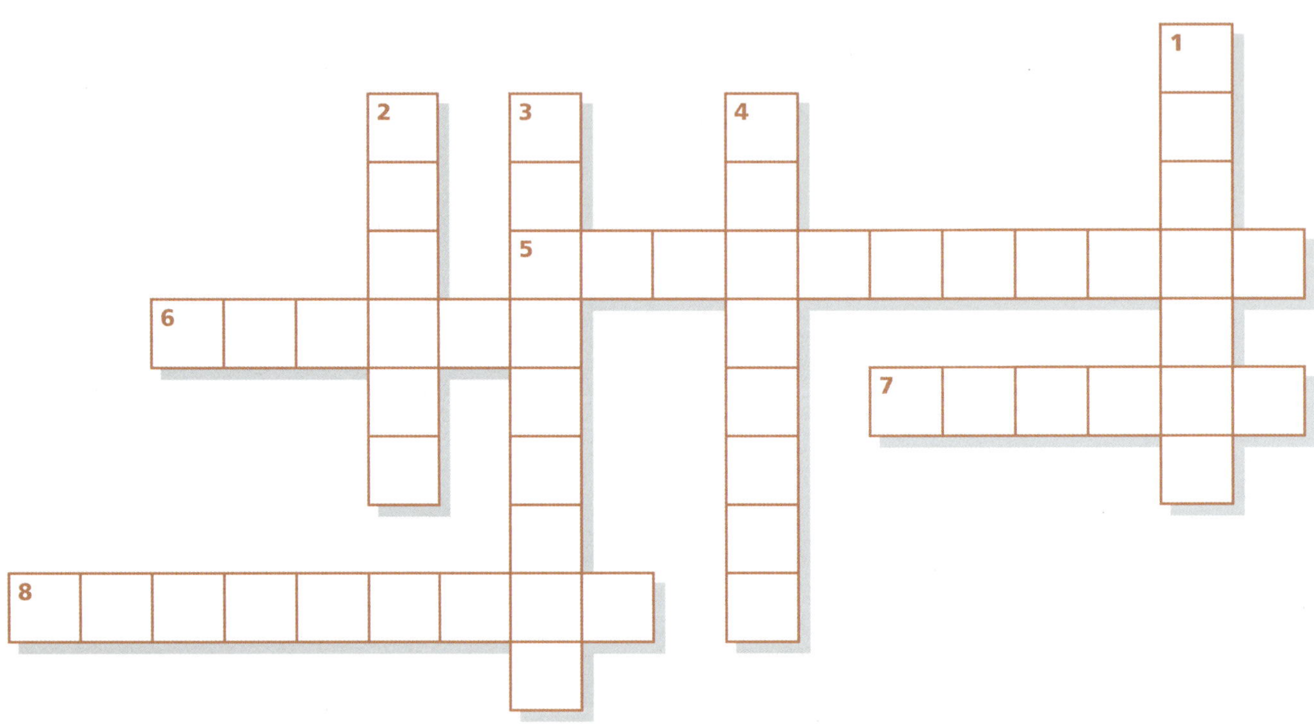

Across →

5. to take part in doing an activity
6. a machine that is made to be used for some special purpose
7. the way something is organized
8. the plot of a story

Down ↓

1. at the center; being the most important part of something
2. a number of things that come one after the other
3. a link that takes you to a web page when you click it
4. to do things together with another person or thing

COMPREHENSION CHECK

Choose and write the right answer for each question.

> Will soon be the only way to read stories and books.
> A new way to enjoy reading stories and books
> Text that talks aloud to the reader   It allows the story to go different ways.
> There is only one ending to the story.   Readers can learn more about the characters.

1. What is hypertext literature?

____

2. What is a feature of printed literature?

____

3. What does a link do within story text?

____

4. What is interesting about J. K. Rowling's hypertext novel?

____

SUMMARY

Complete the summary. Not all the words will be used.

formats	devices	participate	series
central	interact	hyperlinks	storyline

    A fun way to enjoy stories and books is through hypertext literature. By using electronic **1** _________________, readers can interact with **2** _________________ in a story. Readers **3** _________________ throughout the story instead of reading it from start to finish. Stories can be put together in different **4** _________________ using hypertext literature. One type has a central **5** _________________. Links allow the story to go different ways and readers can **6** _________________ with it. Readers eventually return to the main storyline. *Pottermore* is J. K. Rowling's hypertext novel. It is part of the *Harry Potter* **7** _________________. The links help readers understand more about the other *Harry Potter* books.

Types of Writing

VOCABULARY CHECK

Complete the puzzle.

Across ➡

3. something important that happens
5. a series of parts that come together to make the story in a novel, movie, etc.
6. a daily or weekly journal of current events
7. a feeling a person can have

Down ⬇

1. to be made up of
2. a true piece of information
4. a weekly or monthly publication which has articles and photos
5. the reason why something is done

COMPREHENSION CHECK

Choose and write the right answer for each question.

Tell the actors what to do	Facts about a topic	Lines and stanzas
A purpose	Setting	Characters

1. What does the format of writing depend on?

   ____

2. What is a poem made up of?

   ____

3. What does an article contain?

   ____

4. What is the place where the story happens called?

   ____

SUMMARY

Complete the summary. Not all the words will be used.

emotions	contains	plot	facts
events	newspaper	magazine	purposes

In writing, different formats are used for different ❶ _______________. These formats look different and make the readers think and feel different things. Poetry is one format, which mixes language and ❷ _______________. A novel is a book that usually ❸ _______________ characters. Novels have a(n) ❹ _______________, and a sequence of ❺ _______________. These all come together to make the storyline. An article is another format. It gives information and is often found in a(n) ❻ _______________ or a magazine. It contains ❼ _______________ about the topic. Take the time to read different formats in literature so that you can enjoy different things.

VOCABULARY CHECK

Complete the puzzle.

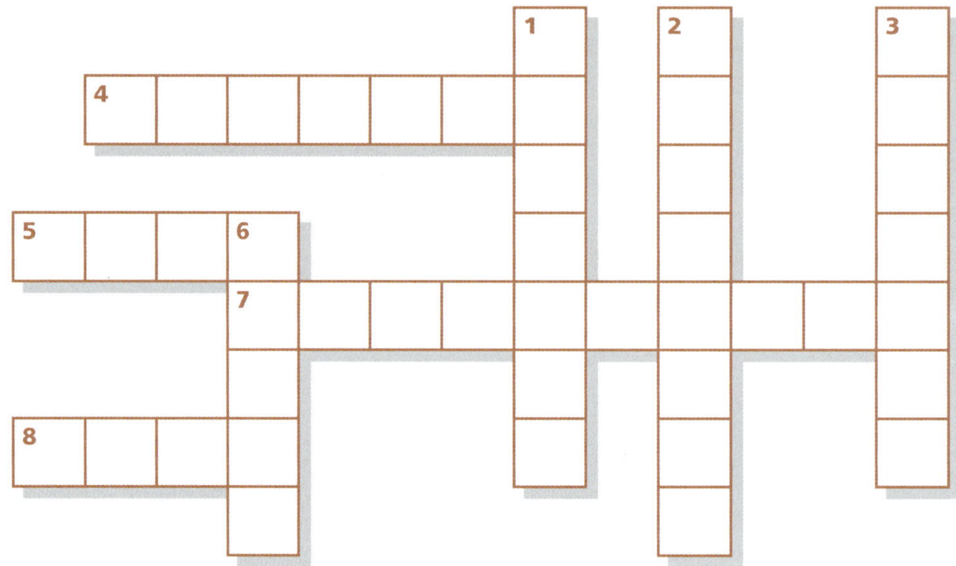

Across →

4. the top part of something
5. after the usual or expected time
7. to value something
8. part of the ground outside where plants can grow

Down ↓

1. to think about deeply
2. to think about something carefully before deciding
3. a short, popular saying that gives advice
6. before the usual or expected time

COMPREHENSION CHECK

Choose and write the right answer for each question.

It might get eaten.	It will probably be safe.
To see what the day will be like	They will get good things before others.
To show a short poem can be interesting	They help people think and feel differently.

1. Why do most people think it's good to wake up early?

   ____

2. What can happen to a worm that goes to top of the soil?

   ____

3. What can happen to a worm that stays under the earth's surface?

   ____

4. How can poems help people?

   ____

SUMMARY

Complete the summary. Not all the words will be used.

late	surface	proverb	early
soil	consider	reflect	understand

Poems help people think and feel different things. This is good because it helps people **①** _______________ themselves better. A good example of this is a poem by Shel Silverstein. It's about a well-known **②** _______________: "The **③** _______________ bird catches the worm." This proverb tells us that we'll get good things before others who are **④** _______________. The poem makes us **⑤** _______________ what happens to the worm in the proverb. The poet makes us **⑥** _______________ on this with his writing. A worm that is living under the ground and comes up to the **⑦** _______________ early in the morning is in danger of getting eaten by a bird.

A Positive Thinker: *Anne of Green Gables*

VOCABULARY CHECK

Complete the puzzle.

1. NOPRAH

2. DELREYL
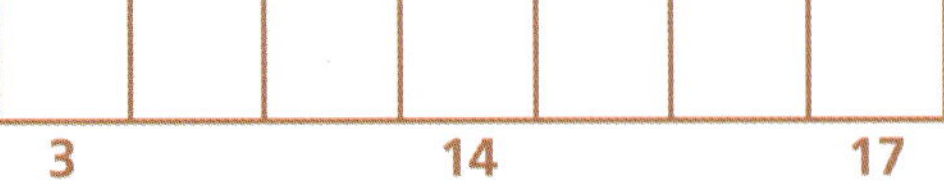

3. NIEDOISATPDP
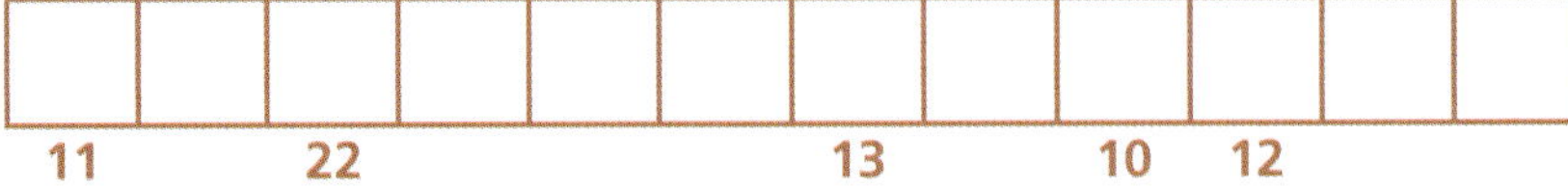

4. AEVRRI

5. SEINADT
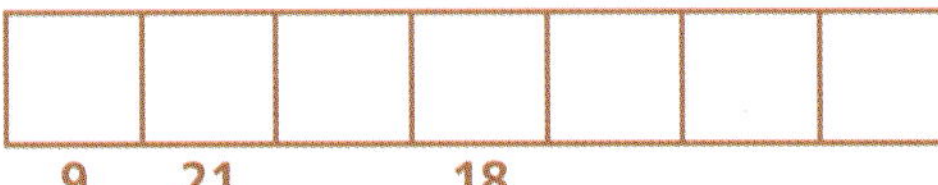

6. VISTOIPE
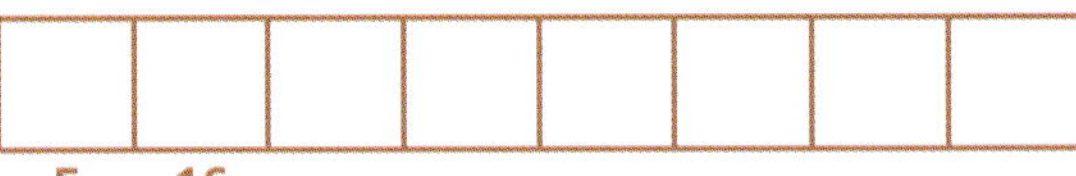

7. TETTUADI
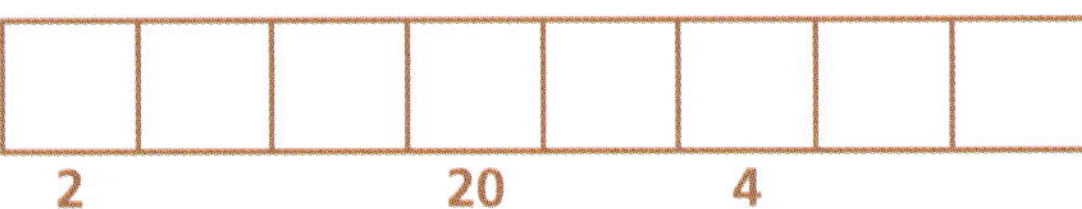

8. FYMRIL
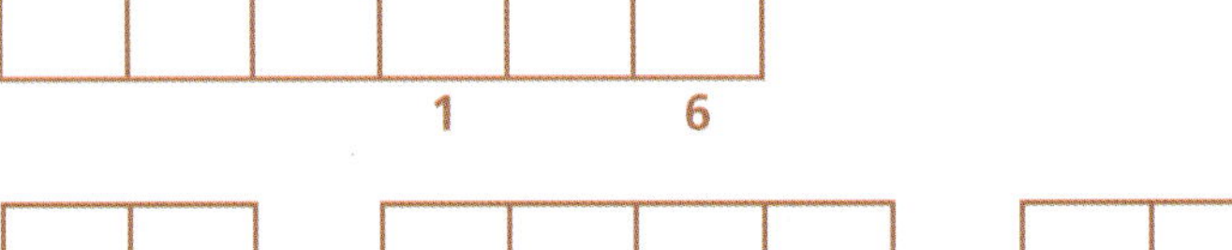

1. a child who has no parents
2. a polite way to say "old"
3. sad or unhappy because something was not as good as you hoped
4. to reach a place you are going to
5. used to say that one thing is done or chosen over another choice
6. thinking of the good side of things
7. a way you think or feel that you show in your actions
8. strongly; not in a weak or uncertain way

COMPREHENSION CHECK

Choose and write the right answer for each question.

Anne talks too much.	They are filled with love.
Bright red hair and freckles	Finding the good in any situation
They needed help on the farm.	They thought Anne was interesting.

1. Why did Matthew and Marilla want to adopt a boy?

   ____

2. Why did Matthew and Marilla change their minds about sending Anne back?

   ____

3. What does Anne's positive attitude help her?

   ____

4. How does Matthew and Marilla's decision to keep Anne change all of their lives?

   ____

SUMMARY

Complete the summary. Not all the words will be used.

elderly	arrives	firmly	disappointed
orphan	attitude	instead	positive

Anne of Green Gables was written by L. M. Montgomery. It is the story about a(n)
1 _______________ girl who helps change the lives of people around her. The story
begins with a(n) **2** _______________ man, Matthew, and woman, Marilla. They live
together on their farm, called Green Gables. They want to adopt a boy, so they are
3 _______________ when a girl arrives **4** _______________. Anne has a(n)
5 _______________ attitude, and she can find the good in any situation. Anne says,
"You can always enjoy things if you make up your mind **6** _______________ that you
will." Matthew and Marilla like Anne's **7** _______________ so much that they decide to
have her stay at Green Gables.

9 Digital Money

VOCABULARY CHECK

Complete the puzzle.

Across →

1. a special piece of plastic used for paying for things
3. a way of doing something
4. safety
5. a piece of paper that is used to make a payment to someone using the money in a bank account
6. more and more

Down ↓

1. money in the form of bills and coins
2. not long ago
5. money in the form of small, flat, and usually round pieces of metal

COMPREHENSION CHECK

Choose and write the right answer for each question.

> Checks and coins   Cards and online banking
> Smartphones   Security
> Get, save, and spend money without ever seeing or touching it
> Usually carry around cash, checks, coins, and cards to pay for things

1. What made people carry less paper money and coins?

   ____

2. What are people worrying about for crypto-currency?

   ____

3. What should be carried around to use online payment services such as PayPal?

   ____

4. What can people do with digital money?

   ____

SUMMARY

Complete the summary. Not all the words will be used.

> methods   recently   cash   checks
> security   coins   increasingly   cards

People usually pay for things with cash, **1** ___________________, **2** ___________________, and cards. They have used these **3** ___________________ to pay for things for a very long time. However, **4** ___________________, people carry around less **5** ___________________, checks, and coins than before. **6** ___________________, people are using only cards and online banking. Another type of digital money is through online payment companies, such as PayPal. Very recently, an even newer form of digital money has emerged called crypto-currency. The number of people and business who accept digital money is increasing, but people are worried about **7** ___________________. They want to be sure their digital money is safe.

VOCABULARY CHECK

Complete the puzzle.

Across →

3. to give something and get something back
4. work done by an individual or group
6. to bring a plan, system, or product into use for the first time
7. how important, useful, or expensive something is
8. during every part of

Down ↓

1. allowing you to do something easily or without trouble
2. something you can sell for money
5. to mark by pressing a design onto the surface

COMPREHENSION CHECK

Choose and write the right answer for each question.

Their value	About 3,300 years ago
Around 800 CE	They exchanged goods.
Most people need it.	A simple way to pay for things

1. How did people first get things they needed?

____

2. What makes a commodity valuable?

____

3. What do coins have stamped onto them?

____

4. When was the first paper money made?

____

SUMMARY

Complete the summary. Not all the words will be used.

introduced	stamped	exchanged	services
throughout	value	commodities	transport

Over time, humans have tried to make paying for things easier. How we pay for things has changed a lot **1** _________________ history. A long time ago, people **2** _________________ goods and **3** _________________ to pay for things. So, eventually **4** _________________ became money. Commodities are things that most people need, such as cows, plants, salt, and cloth. Then, about, 3,300 years ago, metal coins were **5** _________________ as money. The **6** _________________ of each coin was **7** _________________ on it. Coins made paying for things easier. Around 800 CE, paper money was made. Today, people still use paper money and coins, as well as cards and digital money.

VOCABULARY CHECK

Complete the puzzle.

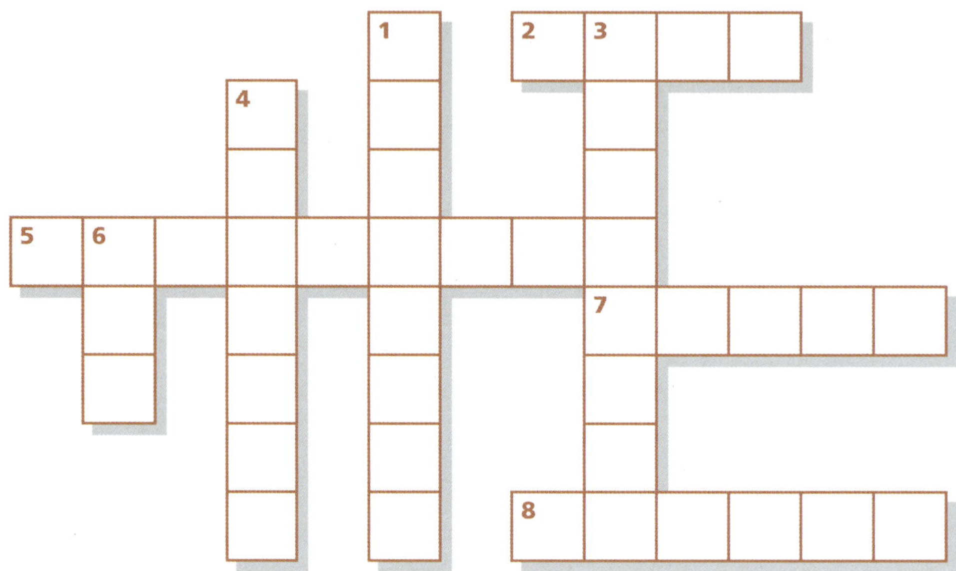

Across ➜

2. to give a job to someone and pay them for doing work
5. to work together
7. one of the parts of a business that shows the value of the company
8. money that is made in a business

Down ↓

1. to grow in size, amount, number, etc.
3. a person who uses their money to make more money
4. to make someone or something better
6. to have something that belongs to you

COMPREHENSION CHECK

Choose and write the right answer for each question.

Create newer and better goods	Business	Stocks
To make profits	At the stock market	At a stock store

1. Where can someone buy shares of a company?

____

2. Why do investors buy stocks?

____

3. What can companies who have many investors do?

____

4. What do we call the small parts of a company that people can buy and sell?

____

SUMMARY

Complete the summary. Not all the words will be used.

own	investors	increase	profits
improve	valuable	stock	cooperate

Stocks are small parts of a company that people can buy, **①** ________________, and sell. Businesses and people go to the **②** ________________ market to **③** ________________ and try to make money together. Some people's goal is to buy a stock and wait for its value to **④** ________________. Then they sell it later for **⑤** ________________. These people are called **⑥** ________________. Investors can sell their stocks at any time. Companies use money from investors to **⑦** ________________ their company and make it more valuable. This is how companies and investors work together to try to make profits in the stock market.

VOCABULARY CHECK

Complete the puzzle.

1. to buy
5. required to be paid or returned by a certain date
6. to take and use something that belongs to someone else for a period of time before returning it
7. a note showing the amount of money that must be paid for something
8. on the most important or simple level

2. able to be trusted to do what is best
3. a secret set of numbers and letters that allows someone to use a computer system
4. extra money you pay if you borrow money

COMPREHENSION CHECK

Choose and write the right answer for each question.

> Adults who earn money
> Most people have at least one credit card.
> Credit card companies remind users to be careful with their cards.
> The owner of the card should pay in small amounts over time with interest.
>
> In about thirty days
> People put their cards in a machine.

1. How do people buy goods using a credit card offline?

   ____

2. When does the amount that is due usually have to be paid?

   ____

3. What may happen when the amount that is due is not fully paid?

   ____

4. Who can usually get a credit card?

   ____

SUMMARY

Complete the summary. Not all the words will be used.

due	interest	purchase	bill
responsible	borrow	fundamental	password

It's important to understand how credit cards work so that people can be
1 _______________ with their money. When a person uses a credit card, they
2 _______________ the credit company's money. The amount of money that the
credit company lends must be paid back by the person who owns the credit card. The
amount that is **3** _______________ must be paid in full or in small amounts over time
with **4** _______________. When the card is used offline, the credit company pays the
5 _______________. To **6** _______________ things online, people type in their
card number, **7** _______________, and other information.

The Math of Faces

VOCABULARY CHECK

Complete the puzzle.

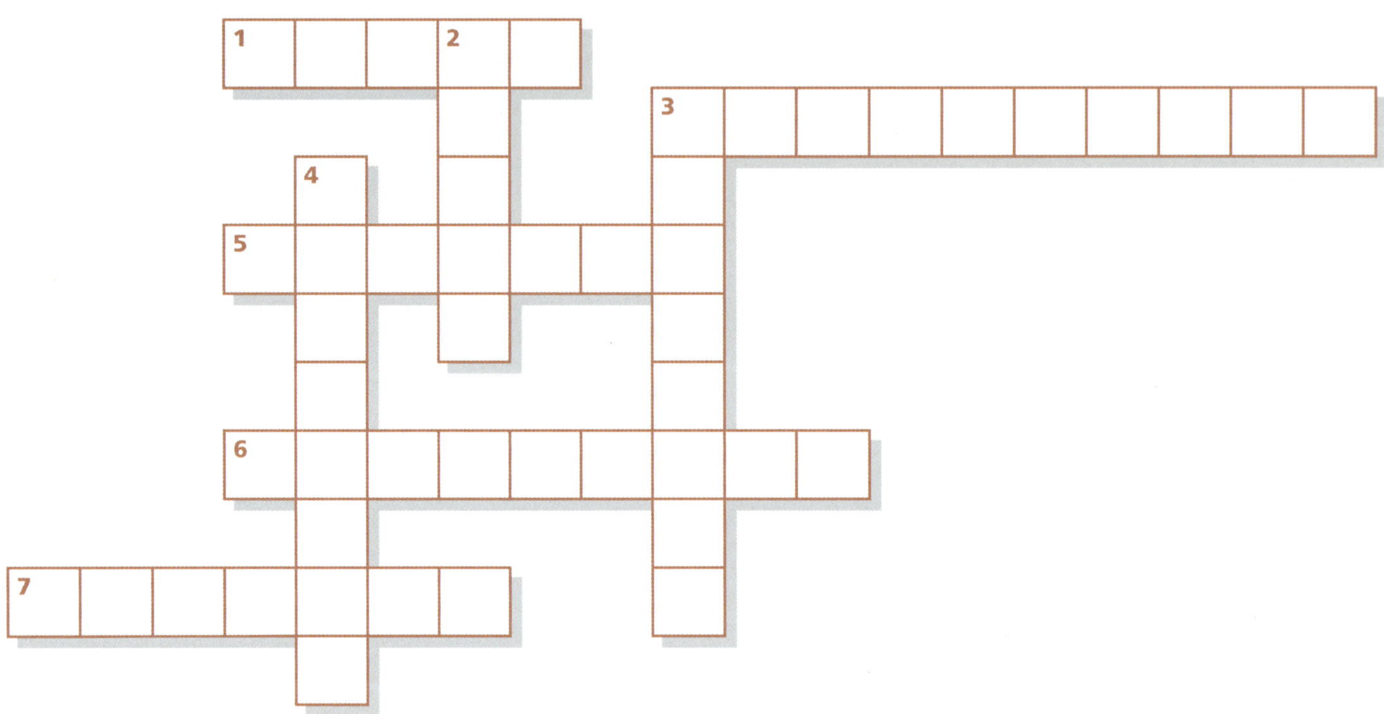

Across →

1. a large group of people
3. related to just one member or part of a larger group
5. a part of something that makes it special
6. to know someone or something
7. a set of instructions that tells a computer what to do

Down ↓

2. how wide something is
3. to pick out or select
4. a type of math that deals with points, lines, angles, surfaces, shapes, and sizes

COMPREHENSION CHECK

Choose and write the right answer for each question.

> Eyes and noses   Studying shapes and sizes
> Identify people in a crowd Facial geometry
> Distance between friends   A person's individual profile

1. What does the facial recognition program make after finishing measurements?

   ____

2. What is geometry?

   ____

3. What can be used to exactly measure facial features?

   ____

4. What can face recognition programs do?

   ____

SUMMARY

Complete the summary. Not all the words will be used.

> geometry   individual   width   features
> crowd   identify   programs   recognize

Almost everyone has different facial **1** _________________. Computer
2 _________________ can recognize the differences in people's faces, such as the shape
of their nose, and the size and shape of their faces. These computer programs record the
3 _________________ of the human face. Facial geometry measures things such as the
exact distance between the eyes, the size of the eyes, the **4** _________________ of the
mouth and nose, and more. Together these measurements make a person's
5 _________________ profile. Facial recognition programs can **6** _________________
people in a(n) **7** _________________. They are used for security at airports and other
important places.

14 Cooking with Math

VOCABULARY CHECK

Complete the puzzle.

Across →

1. difficult to do or deal with
4. to make or become twice as much
5. to give help
6. a food product that is made from a bean and used to add a good flavor to food
7. especially
8. a room where food is cooked

Down ↓

2. something you work out using math
3. related to cooking

COMPREHENSION CHECK

Choose and write the right answer for each question.

One cup	Two cups	Math
Three eggs	Four eggs	How to add fractions

1. What can we use to help us use recipes to cook?

   ____

2. How many cups of flour do you need to make 20 cookies?

   ____

3. What do you have to know to make 20 cookies from recipe for 10 cookies?

   ____

4. How many eggs do you need for 30 cookies?

   ____

SUMMARY

Complete the summary. Not all the words will be used.

aid	double	tricky	particularly
culinary	kitchen	fractions	calculations

Math can **1** _______________ us in real life, **2** _______________ in the kitchen. For instance, if you wanted to make cookies for twenty people but the recipe you have only makes ten cookies you can use math to help you. Just add **3** _______________ to **4** _______________ the recipe. Adding fractions can help with those **5** _______________ culinary **6** _______________. For example, if the recipe says you need ½ cup of sugar just do the math to double it. So, ½ + ½ = 2/2, and 2/2 = 1. So, you need 1 cup of sugar. Remember that math is easy to use in the **7** _______________.

VOCABULARY CHECK

Complete the puzzle.

Across →

2. a measurement of distance in the imperial system
6. used to say that something is sad or has bad luck
8. a part of the government that is responsible for doing a particular job

Down ↓

1. very much or by a lot of people
3. at the present time; now
4. problems
5. a measurement of weight in the imperial system
7. to do badly or not succeed

COMPREHENSION CHECK

Choose and write the right answer for each question.

It finally get to the Mars.	It's easier to work with other countries.
The metric system	It is more accurate than the imperial system.
The imperial system	It crashed. It took a year.

1. What form of measurement is used in America?

   ____

2. Why does NASA use metric measurements?

   ____

3. Which system of measurement is used in most of the world?

   ____

4. What happened to the spaceship?

   ____

SUMMARY

Complete the summary. Not all the words will be used.

trouble	miles	agency	unfortunately
failed	pounds	widely	currently

The metric system and the imperial system are the two **1** ________________ used systems of measurement in the world. The imperial system is older than the metric system. **2** ________________, most of the world uses the metric system. It uses measurements like kilometers and kilograms. However, some countries still use the imperial system. It uses measurements like **3** ________________ and **4** ________________. America uses the imperial system, but **5** ________________ this caused trouble for the American space **6** ________________, NASA. NASA used the metric system to build a spaceship. One of the American companies made a computer program for the spaceship using imperial measurements. As a result, the spaceship crashed and the mission **7** ________________.

VOCABULARY CHECK

Complete the puzzle.

Across →

3. original or clever
5. close in value or amount but not exact
6. a best guess of the size, value, amount, etc.
7. something you use to help you do work
8. to bring things together

Down ↓

1. to understand or solve something
2. the size and shape of something
4. doing something by hand, without electricity

COMPREHENSION CHECK

Choose and write the right answer for each question.

By using a measuring tape or a scale	To measure big animals
The proportions of a whale	They help estimate the length and weight.
To make great inventions	The way of living of animals

1. Why do scientists need to be creative?

____

2. How can scientists get manual measurements?

____

3. What do scientists know after studying so many dead animals?

____

4. How are pictures helpful to scientists?

____

SUMMARY

Complete the summary. Not all the words will be used.

creative	manual	approximate	estimate
tool	collecting	figure out	proportions

Some things are easy to measure if you use a simple **1** _______________ and read the measurement. However, a big animal like a whale can't be measured easily. So, scientists need to find **2** _______________ ways to measure these big animals. To measure whales, scientists usually start by studying dead ones. Scientists do **3** _______________ measurements of these animals. After measuring many dead whales and **4** _______________ lots of information, scientists can **5** _______________ the approximate **6** _______________ of a whale. Scientists try to collect as much information as they can about the animal and then they make a(n) **7** _______________ of the length and weight of it.

Memo

Memo

Memo

Memo

Memo

READING FUTURE

Reading Future Change is a three-level reading series for beginner to intermediate learners of English. Each level has three books that increase students' reading skills. Each book contains nonfiction passages covering a broad range of school subjects on high-interest topics linked to the future. Reading comprehension is progressively developed with fluency. Students gradually expand their vocabulary through exposure to high-frequency and practical vocabulary related to the unit topics. Students will develop 21st Century Skills and shape the future with ***Reading Future***.

Features

★ Informative passages covering various fields related to the future
★ Interesting topics covering a wide range of subjects, including social studies, science, geography, math, economics, history, art, music, literature, language arts, physical education, and more
★ Reading skill exercises to develop ability to understand the structure of the passages through graphic organizers
★ Projects based around 21st Century Skills
★ Colorful images which show real-life topics and situations

Connect 1-3 **Change 1-3** **Create 1-3**

Components

★ Student Book and workbook
★ Project page introduction video
★ Supplemental Materials
Online materials, including Answer Keys, can be found here:
www.compasspub.com/RFChange2

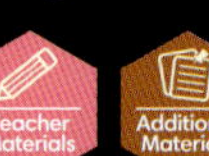